SUGAR FREE SAXOPHONE

The Life and Music of

Jackie McLean

Front cover photo:

Francis Wolff's photo of Jackie taken at his January 18th 1959 *Jackie's Bag* Blue Note session is one of his best, famous for hardly ever having been seen. Only three tracks were recorded on that day and the LP was not issued until more than a year later when three new pieces were recorded. Then, on October 26th 1961, McLean recorded *A Fickle Sonance* and Blue Note's designer, Reid Miles, used a small part of the photo, the top part of Jackie's head showing him holding his hat, and no more. Wolff was reportedly annoyed at Miles regularly chopping up his photos and using only bits of them, often clipping off the top of a musician's head. The complete picture has been one of my favourite photographs of Jackie McLean since I first saw it in an Artists Collective magazine and I particularly wanted it as the cover picture for this book. I often refer to it as the *Jackie's Bag* picture although it never appeared on any LP or CD edition of that album. I am grateful to Michael Cuscuna for the use of the cover photos.

D. A.

SUGAR FREE SAXOPHONE

The Life and Music of Jackie McLean

Derek Ansell

Published by Northway Publications
39 Tytherton Road, London N19 4PZ, UK.
www.northwaybooks.com

Copyright © 2012, Derek Ansell.

The right of Derek Ansell to be identified as author of this work has been asserted by him in accordance with the Copyright, Designs and Patents Act 1988.

All rights reserved. No part of this book may be reproduced, stored in a retrieval system or transmitted, in any form or by any means without prior permission in writing of the publisher, nor be otherwise circulated in any form of binding or cover other than that in which it is published and without a similar condition including this condition being imposed on the subsequent purchaser.

Cover design by Adam Yeldham, Raven Design.

Cover photos by Francis Wolff © Mosaic Images LLC.

A CIP record for this book is available from the British Library.

ISBN 978 0 9557888 6 4

First edition 2012

Printed and bound in Great Britain by CPI Antony Rowe, Chippenham, Wiltshire.

Author Derek Ansell at an event in his home town of Newbury, Berkshire, with his book about the music of Hank Mobley, April 2008.

Derek Ansell writes regular reviews of live jazz and classical music for magazines and newspapers and has contributed more than two hundred articles and numerous interviews, record and book reviews to *Jazz Journal International*. He is the author of *Workout: The Music of Hank Mobley* (Northway, 2008) and a book about the music of John Coltrane (Flipped Eye, forthcoming). He has also written three novels (two published and one forthcoming).

CONTENTS

	ACKNOWLEDGEMENTS	ix
1.	TIME WARP ONE: SITTING IN FOR THE BIRD	1
2.	SUGAR HILL, HARLEM	5
3.	OUT OF THE BLUE	12
4.	STARTING AS HE MEANT TO GO ON	19
5.	ISN'T JACKIE McLEAN IN THERE SOMEWHERE?	25
6.	THE JAZZ LIFE	33
7.	THE SHAPING OF A MAJOR SOLOIST	40
8.	BLUE NOTE BEGINNINGS	46
9.	THE CONNECTION	52
10.	BLUESNIK	59
11.	NEW DIRECTIONS AND OLD STANDBYS	63
12.	ONE STEP FORWARD, ONE STEP BACK	71
13.	ONE STEP BEYOND	79
14.	DESTINATION – OUT	87
15.	ACTION	94
16.	NEW AND OLD GOSPEL	104
17.	TEACHING	110
18.	MUSICIAN, SOLOIST, EDUCATOR, ACTIVIST	117
19.	THE ARTISTS COLLECTIVE	126
20.	LATE FLOURISHES	132

21.	TIME WARP TWO: PARKER'S MOOD	138
22.	RHYTHM OF THE EARTH	142
23.	WORKING MUSICIAN	151
24.	THE SOUND OF JAZZ	155
25.	TIME WARP THREE: FAREWELL ONE	162
26.	FAREWELL TWO	166
27.	FAREWELL THREE	172
28.	THE LEGACY ONE: THE RECORDS	177
29.	THE LEGACY TWO	189
30.	NOTES	193
31.	RECOMMENDED RECORDS	199
31.	INDEX	203

ACKNOWLEDGEMENTS

This book about Jackie McLean was inspired first and foremost by the music he made, in particular the recordings, some of them great classics of the art of jazz. My thanks are due to Jackie's wife Dollie and daughter Melonae who sent me cuttings from magazines, literature from the Artists Collective and a copy of the film *Jackie McLean on Mars*. I am also indebted to ex-McLean student, saxophonist Steve Lehman, for his article in *Critical Studies in Improvisation* and to various writers about jazz, notably Ira Gitler, Gary Giddins and A. B. Spellman. Ken Burns generously gave his permission to quote from the transcript of his film *Jazz*. Closer to home my thanks are due to Ann and Roger Cotterrell for their support and comprehensive editing, and a special thank you to my wife Sarah for her support and understanding when I enter the world of writing and seem oblivious to everything else going on around me. Most of all, my thanks are due to the subject himself, John (Jackie) Lenwood McLean, who, whether talking to writers in jazz magazines, on radio, television or on Ken Burns' mammoth television show, *Jazz*, always told it straight with no punches pulled. I hope I have managed to do the same in presenting his story.

I

TIME WARP: ONE
SITTING IN FOR THE BIRD

The young man coming out of the Subway at Houston Street in New York City, looking very smart in a blue suit with a white shirt and a tie, is a young musician named Jackie McLean. It is 1949, a few years after the end of World War Two, and bebop, as it is commonly known, is the new jazz sensation, the modern sound of jazz that most youngsters are listening to, and a few, like young McLean, have been learning to play. He is eighteen years old and a particularly good player on the instrument for one so young. So good, in fact, that he was heard playing in a band a short time ago by alto saxophonist Charlie Parker, known as 'Bird', the main soloist and principal innovative force in the new modern jazz. That is why he is emerging from the subway now, en route to Chateau Gardens where drummer Art Blakey and a combo of modern jazz musicians will be arriving shortly to begin their first set.

Earlier that day young Jackie had arrived home to find his mother in a state of excitement, telling him that although she didn't think he was going to believe it, Charlie Parker had been on the phone. The young man had eagerly demanded to know what the message from Bird was. Parker had asked that Jackie should wear a blue suit, go down to Chateau Gardens and play for him until he arrived, later in the evening.

After the initial shock, the excitement and then the first flush of pleasure had subsided a little, Jackie had spent the rest of the afternoon practising on his alto sax and then, dressing slowly and meticulously, had taken the subway to Houston Street for Chateau Gardens, a place where they played jazz and dances in downtown Manhattan.

Now, once inside the Gardens he approaches the bandstand eagerly, if nervously, and waits for Art Blakey, who knows him, to arrive.... He is, in his eagerness and excitement, the first to get there. This is a big day indeed for the young saxophonist. Parker does not easily, or indeed usually, send in subs to play for him until he arrives; more often than not he just gets there late or when he is ready or forgets the gig altogether but, when he does put a sub in, it is always an experienced, older player who has played around the scene for years and years. Parker must have a high regard for this youngster.

When Blakey and the other musicians arrive, Jackie gives the drummer Parker's message and Art says 'OK.' He knows Parker well and he's seen and heard young Jackie McLean playing in bars around town and knows that this is what Bird wants. He announces to the audience that Parker has been delayed but he will be there later to play – and meantime, this young musician named Jackie McLean is going to play. Many years later, McLean confided to historian Ken Burns that he could feel the disappointment rippling through the audience as Art made his announcement, but it could not put the young man off; this was his big opportunity and he was going to take full advantage of it. With the master's blessing.

He begins to play with the band, calling the tunes in Parker's absence but with Blakey's approval. He plays 'Confirmation', 'A Night in Tunisia' and then 'Now's the Time' and the ballad 'Don't Blame Me'. These are all compositions very familiar to Charlie Parker, items that he plays regularly and selections that Jackie has played over and over again, trying to get that elusive, cutting Parker sound, that hip bebop phrasing that all the young alto players are attempting to emulate. Maybe, even as early as this, there is the hint, just a hint of a personal sound beginning to filter through, a sound tinged with the blues, perhaps a shade sharp, something that will become a personal attribute in his later playing but not yet audible to the average jazz fan in the 1940s.

Jackie McLean was always a forceful, assertive young musician, even in his earliest days but at this time, with the all-pervasive influence of Parker on every modern jazz musician, it is that sound that predominates, in his phrasing, in his main attack, in his rhythmic approach. In any case, he is anxious to play Parker tunes that the audience will be familiar with and enjoy hearing. The bebop anthems are familiar to the audience to the extent that they often hum the opening melodies at the start of each selection. Jackie is playing wild bop, tearing it up, fashioning new phrases, swinging, and riding exhilaratingly on top of Blakey's cymbal beat.

He is enjoying himself immensely, running through the chord changes, hearing the surging lift that a rhythm section with Art Blakey in it gives to every soloist. Then there is a sudden surge of people at the back of the stage and, as Jackie looks up and notes the dense mass of the crowds, he sees a saxophone case being raised up high and another surge of people. They follow the newly arrived Charlie Parker all the way down to the bandstand and stand there jostling eagerly, waiting for him to get up there and start playing. But Parker, taking his time in leisurely fashion, signals up to young Jackie to keep playing, which he does. Bird gets himself on the stage, takes out his horn, adjusts it, fixes his reed, as Jackie prepares to pack up his instrument and depart. Parker smiles at his protégé and says 'Play one with me,' so the two saxophonists join forces as Blakey begins to stoke up fires in the rhythm section and drive the two soloists forward. Parker is a hero in the community at that time and everything he plays is listened to in awed silence by the audience. The sheer excitement of being on the same stage, in the same band as Parker is almost overwhelming for Jackie McLean. But he's enjoying every minute of it.

Finally, it is time for Parker to take full control and command of his combo and get down to the serious business of playing bebop, getting some modern jazz cooking in earnest. He smiles at Jackie and tells him to go and sit out front and he will see him later. Jackie is soon so immersed in the music of Parker and the band that he almost, but not quite, forgets why he is there. Parker plays brilliantly, far into the night and, at the end, he seeks out Jackie, who is still there in the audience, tapping his toes and nodding his head, and gives him $15, a lot of money for a gig at that time. It is a great night and a defining moment for Jackie McLean of Sugar Hill, Harlem. It is possibly the first indication that he will have a long and distinguished career in jazz, in music of quality, and something that he will remember and recount many long years after the event.

2

SUGAR HILL, HARLEM

The Sugar Hill district of Harlem in New York City is bounded by 155th Street in the north and 145th Street in the south. The area looks out over Manhattan from high up, giving views of the Harlem River. Jackie McLean lived in this district from the age of twelve, surrounded by young people who would also become jazz soloists. An early neighbourhood band featured him with two saxophonists, Sonny Rollins and Andy Kirk Jr., and the pianist Kenny Drew. Another local was drummer Art Taylor. He became friendly with Rollins early on, as did Richie Powell and later his brother Bud. The area had always been a haven for artists and jazz musicians and it was here that Billie Holiday often appeared, along with Duke Ellington, Arnett Cobb, Don Redman, Nat King Cole and many others.

Many years later, Jackie would refer to himself as a 'sugar free saxophonist' and commentators were never quite sure whether he was referring to his direct, hard sound on the saxophone or his home area. He often referred to himself as being lucky to grow up with all those great musicians on his doorstep, sometimes quite literally, and especially with pianist Bud Powell. Powell had been the major soloist in the bop revolution in the early 1940s and an important innovative force on his instrument, along with Parker on alto sax and trumpeter Dizzy Gillespie. Powell obviously heard something in the young McLean's playing and helped him by showing him different chords and giving him instruction. Jackie was only fifteen when he began meeting up with Powell and had been playing alto sax just for a year or two. This would have been in 1946 and it was shortly afterwards that young McLean started playing truant from school, putting his school books in a subway lock-up and heading down to the Apollo theatre to hear Parker play.

John Lenwood (Jackie) McLean was born in NYC on May 17th 1931 and, although some sources claim his birth date to be 1932, his widow, Dollie McLean, confirmed the 1931 date. He grew up listening to people like Coleman Hawkins, Count Basie and, through Basie's orchestra, the early solos of Lester Young. Young seems to have been an early and very important influence, a man who, Jackie felt, was the one who really started bebop, or modern jazz. As he put it in his interview with Ken Burns, talking about Billie Holiday's recordings that feature Lester Young solos, 'You'll hear, back as early as 1937, '38, '39, his style was already developing beyond what the music sounded like before that. There were a lot of eighth notes ... and the two feel was beginning to disappear, and a lot of triplets and grace notes.' Jackie went on to point out that Lester's sound was much lighter than that of Coleman Hawkins who had a 'deep, velvety vibrato'.[1] Young had a lot less vibrato and this, in turn, influenced Charlie Parker who took it much further and then, when he met up with Dizzy Gillespie and Thelonious Monk, helped to develop this wonderful music.

Jackie claimed Parker, Lester Young, Dexter Gordon, and Sonny Rollins as his favourite saxophonists in the early years but it was Bud Powell that he claimed as his main influence. It was to Powell's house that he would head after school to study, to learn and to jam. It was at some point later that Young became a major influence, almost as strong as Parker. Jackie talked about bebop and what the word meant to him on several occasions, and was convinced that Young was the originator. Evolving out of his concept and his solos, Jackie felt that the way Lester played, from when he was with Count Basie in the 1930s, was the beginning of bop soloing and he often quoted a phrase

Young played on 'I Never Knew', a phrase that came before the melody.

So young McLean listened to jazz at home in Harlem. He had little recollection of his father John McLean Sr. who died when he was just seven years old. John Sr. had been a jazz guitarist of some stature having played with swing musicians like Tiny Bradshaw and saxophonist Teddy Hill. He is reported to have locked himself and his son in a room, sat him up on a dresser and played the guitar to him. Jackie's mother, Alpha Omega McLean, had little time for musicians and Jackie could only remember seeing his father three times. Then, one day in midwinter, John Sr. slipped on ice in the street, hit his head on a curbstone and died in hospital two days later. After that Alpha worked hard as a domestic, bringing her son up on her own, and studying until she qualified as a laboratory technician, although much later she became a schoolteacher.[2]

When Jackie was twelve years old his mother remarried and his new stepfather, Jimmy Briggs, became much more influential and helpful to him than his own father had ever been. Jackie and his mother moved from their home in Washington Heights to live with Briggs at 185th Street and Nicholas Avenue in the Sugar Hill district. Briggs owned a record shop at 141st Street and Eighth Avenue which specialised in jazz, and young Jackie would soon start to work there, selling albums by day and in the evening shutting up shop and retiring to a back room to study and listen to the latest jazz releases. Jackie's mother had referred to his father as 'a no good musician' and at first opposed his interest in learning to play an instrument but he must have talked her round at some point and she capitulated. He also worked on his godfather, Norman Cobbs, who played saxophone in the band at the Abyssinian Baptist Church which the family attended. Cobbs gave him his first instrument, a soprano saxophone, but Jackie was reported to have been disappointed with the soprano and really wanted an alto.

His first alto saxophone, bought for him by his mother, arrived when he was thirteen years old. He linked up to talk, hang out and practise with Rollins, Drew and Taylor and received crucial, priceless help, encouragement and instruction from Bud Powell. By this time he had also started to listen to records by Coleman Hawkins, Ben Webster and Lester Young, brought home for him by Jimmy Briggs.

In the liner notes to his Prestige record *Makin' the Changes*, Jackie tells Nat Hentoff: 'Bud made me play by ear, and taught me a lot about chords. Sometimes I'd come by his house on a Friday afternoon and we'd play, off and on, until Sunday.' McLean admitted that he did not understand or take in everything Powell told him; he was only about sixteen or seventeen at the time. But he is credited with getting young Richie Powell playing the piano, saying angrily to him: 'You're Bud Powell's brother, how can you not play?' Richie had been responsible for introducing Jackie to his brother after the youngster went into Briggs' record shop and told McLean who he was.

Many reports claim that McLean did not learn harmony or theory directly from Powell but that the pianist worked on the young man's ear. Powell would play something on the piano and get Jackie to play the chord changes behind him until he learned to improvise freely around them. After some time and a lot of practice, Powell took Jackie to Birdland with him and during the evening called him up on the bandstand to play. That was an honour for Jackie and he never forgot it. Priceless help, then, from a master although, looking ahead to Jackie's early experience playing and recording with Miles Davis in 1951 to 1956, teaching him to play by ear may have held him back as, according to Davis, the young McLean was lazy and would mostly play by ear. He was reluctant to take the time and trouble to learn popular standard tunes which were, then as now, the backbone of many a modern jazz musician's repertoire.

The neighbourhood friends and acquaintances in the area

where he lived must have been a big help in McLean's early development. He was very friendly with Rollins and played in the tenorist's band as a youngster although by the time he attended the Benjamin Franklin High School, Rollins had just graduated. Feeling that he did not have enough comrades there, Jackie left after one year and switched to the Theodore Roosevelt High School in the Bronx. There he met Andy Kirk Jr., another musical influence. A strong one in fact and, just as Jackie acknowledged that Sonny Rollins was 'eons ahead of me in music', he also conceded that Kirk was even further ahead at that time. According to McLean, Bird used to go to Andy Kirk's house whenever he was in the area. Kirk's development as a youngster had been phenomenal and Jackie remembered that Sonny Stitt and Parker 'used to sit in the room and hear him practice'.[3] Kirk had been a colleague and teacher of both Rollins and McLean but his story was ultimately one of promise unfulfilled. Already, in his teens, he was working on methods to expand and form a personal method of expression on Parker's music, but Rollins began to develop at an almost unbelievable rate himself shortly after this. He went away for nine months and on his return his playing was 'incredible'. Kirk told McLean about the way Rollins sounded and Jackie listened to the new Rollins, 'and what he was doing bowled me over.' After that Kirk began to slide into deep depression and heroin addiction and never played an instrument again.

Jackie had his first job in 1949, after high school graduation, at the Paramount theatre where large-scale music shows were performed. It was only a job as an usher which he had taken in response to pressure from his mother who told him she was not prepared to let him just 'lay around the house all day, living the life of a musician'. Not, at least, until he could earn good money from that sort of life. This would indicate that he made little if any money from playing the saxophone up to that time. The job only lasted two weeks and later Jackie spoke contemptuously about ushering, wearing monkey suits at the Paramount. The 'monkey suits' were obligatory which may have been the main reason the job did not last. By his own admission Jackie was, at this time, a rebellious teenager as well as a young junkie and he found it difficult to keep himself and the suit clean and tidy and stand still for long periods of time. The job had its compensations, however, and while he was there he managed to hear concerts by Teddy Hill and Duke Ellington.

Many years later, Jackie was to claim that he and his friends were all hip junkies at that time but that most of the mothers on the hill went out of their way to give their children good manners. Jackie's mother tried to protect him and make him behave well, pushed him towards what she regarded as suitable jobs and, all the time he lived at home with her, required him to get in at a respectable time of night, even if he had a jazz gig. She even managed to get her son to Agricultural and Technical College in North Carolina thinking it would get him away from the jazz life, jazz people and junk. Jackie found the campus life did not suit him at all, did not join in any of the activities and felt out of place for a whole year. And that was his first and last year: he headed back to NYC and carried on where he had left off. He jammed every minute he could, looked out for every jazz gig going in New York and played with whoever would let him sit in.

As there were so many important musicians growing up with him and attending the same schools, and so many influences to absorb and make use of, the way to becoming a musician was more or less mapped out for McLean by fate alone. There had been several early bouts of truancy to hear Parker playing and, a little later, Parker checked out the bars and cafes where McLean was playing and became more and more impressed by what he heard. But it was trumpeter Miles Davis who gave Jackie his first jazz gig, in 1950, while he was still a teenager and, a little later, his first record date. Bud Powell had arranged for his young friend to sit in with Miles' band at Birdland where the trumpeter had a gig. Jackie, although nervous, arrived at the club, sat in with Miles and must have played fairly well as Davis invited him to come to his house the next day. He also asked Jackie if he had any written music and invited the young man to bring his compositions. 'I don't have them written but I can show them to you,' Jackie replied, indicating that possibly due to his studies with Powell he was already relying heavily on his ear rather than written arrangements. So that was Jackie McLean in 1950, a little unsure of himself, as we shall see, and, it must be said, a little lazy. But he was, at this point, on the brink of a major career as a jazz soloist.

3

OUT OF THE BLUE

On October 5th 1951 Miles Davis had a record date with Prestige in New York City. He had assembled a strong cast of sidemen with Sonny Rollins on tenor, Walter Bishop Jr. on piano, Tommy Potter, bass, the dependable, explosive Art Blakey on drums, and Jackie McLean. This was McLean's first jazz session but not his first recording: that had been made in 1948 at the age of just sixteen with Charlie Singleton's rhythm and blues band (Star 719). On Miles' Prestige date he was the youngest man, playing alto sax, and raring to go. Sleevenote annotator Ira Gitler[1] says Jackie was still in his teens at this session but, if the May 17th 1931 birthday is correct, and it is, he was in fact just twenty years old. Gitler also mentions that this date was the first occasion when Prestige used the new microgroove long playing record format; up until this time all recordings had been 78 shellac discs with a playing time of barely three minutes. *Dig* (Prestige 7012) was one of the earliest chances that jazz musicians had to 'stretch out', to play solos that lasted four, five or even ten minutes in length. From the vantage point of the twenty-first century and digital compact discs, it seems strange to think that McLean's first record date coincided with the start of the long playing vinyl record, a format that was as groundbreaking and important in its day as compact discs in the early 1980s.

This session, though Jackie's first jazz record date, was not without incident. On arrival at the studio he was surprised and a little shocked to see Charlie Parker sitting in the control booth. 'Oh my God,' Jackie said, telling the story many years later, ''cause it made me nervous, you know, just to see him, because I idolised him so much; I think a lot of young musicians did.'[2]

According to Miles Davis' autobiography, Jackie was so nervous that he kept going over to Parker and asking him what he was doing there. Parker just smiled, told him he was playing really well and was cool because he understood what the young man was going through and how he must have felt.

Everybody sounds good on 'Dig', the opening track on the record; Miles thought that he played better on this session than he had for some time, possibly because he was addicted to heroin and felt quite relaxed. Looking at it from a slightly different angle, Sonny Rollins said on a *YouTube* item posted on the internet that he felt that he and Jackie provided the hard bop element on that record that helped to put Miles back in favour with his followers, the hipsters of NYC. Apparently, according to Rollins, many of them had been alienated from Davis due to his *Birth of the Cool* sessions recorded in 1949–50, feeling that this music was too slight and ephemeral to be taken seriously and not the best representation of Miles Davis. Whether Miles agreed or not is open to question but he did in fact move more towards bop and hard bop in his music throughout the 1950s.

In his sleevenote Ira Gitler makes much of the growing partnership between Miles and Sonny Rollins but Jackie's first solo is quite brisk and confident; he opens with a typical Parker attention-grabbing phrase but goes on to play an assured-sounding bop solo. Whatever he was feeling with Parker sitting there listening, his solo playing on the the rest of the session also sounded bright and fairly confident. Charles Mingus had gone with Miles to the studio that day and he played bass on 'Conception', a piece that appeared on a different record of that name, but the regular bassist, Tommy Potter, played on all the other selections. With so much going on, seasoned veterans visiting or occasionally playing, Jackie could well have been overwhelmed and unable to play much at all. He was in fast company with Miles, Rollins, Blakey and Walter Bishop but his solo on 'Denial' oozes confidence and brio. Even if the language is mainly Parker, at least he has a thorough understanding of it and can play it well. But there are, in fact, little tell-tale signs of the emerging Jackie McLean sound to be heard if we listen carefully. He was already playing slightly behind the beat and that rather personal, almost aggressive tone of his was just starting to assert itself. 'Bluing', a typical Miles line of the time has Jackie following a strong Rollins solo with a blues-flecked statement that is strong and inventive and, once again, indicates a personal sound fighting to come through a Parker-styled delivery. 'Out of the Blue' is in lively, happy mode although the tempo is steady, not too fast and not too slow. Jackie sounds relaxed at last and his solo, inventive and flowing, just tumbles out.

He was playing well and the session ended with some good music on the tapes but the next recording session with Miles had other problems for McLean to face up to. It was made in New York on May 9th 1952 at the WOR Studios for Blue Note Records, the best and most respected of the independent record labels and Miles had lined up a sterling bop cast of musicians headed by trombonist J. J. Johnson. The rhythm section consisted of pianist Gil Coggins, bassist Oscar Pettiford and drummer Kenny Clarke. It is immediately apparent that Jackie sounds more relaxed here than on his first date and is obviously not overawed, or indeed overshadowed, by his illustrious colleagues. 'Donna', a fast bop line, was written by McLean even though it is the same song as 'Dig' which was credited to Davis on the Prestige disc. McLean is very assured here and whips through his solo segments with no hesitation whatsoever. If he was reluctant to make the effort to learn to play standards, 'Woody 'n' You' he knew as it was a bop staple and his solo here leaps out of the speakers, his sound strong and tensile, bluish-grey in colour, as he fashions his own variations in a tone that was steadily becoming unique and personal. Miles wanted to record

'Yesterdays' and 'How Deep Is the Ocean' but there were problems: Jackie couldn't get his solo right and claimed that he didn't know the tune of 'Yesterdays'. Miles became angry and cursed him out but things did not improve. When asked what was the matter with him, Jackie said that those tunes were old and from another period and he was a young guy. Miles put him right saying that music had no periods, music is music. 'I like this tune, this is my band, you're in my band, I'm playing this tune, so you learn it and learn all the tunes, whether you like them or not. Learn them.'

In the end Jackie sat out those two tunes and did not play on them but it caused something of an issue between him and Davis. Davis tried to persuade him that he must work hard and learn all the music he was likely to be called on to play and he did make the effort later and became a consummate ballad player and interpreter of standard songs. It was his early nervousness and insecurity that had caused him to hold back on standards, similar behaviour in fact to his nervous reaction to finding Charlie Parker in the studio listening to him play. In any event, in spite of the slight rift caused by this incident, they continued to play music and hang out together during this time.

* * *

It was a hectic and in many ways troublesome four years for McLean between 1951 when he had his first gig with Miles Davis and 1955 when he began to find more confidence in his own ability and a mature approach to his music. At his very first gig with Davis in 1951 at Birdland, one of the leading jazz clubs in NYC, Jackie had played half a solo and suddenly rushed offstage, out into the backyard and been violently sick into a garbage can. It was partly nervousness and partly the desire to do well in a band that contained leading musicians like Rollins, Kenny Drew on piano, Percy Heath on bass and Art Blakey behind the drums. Miles, wondering what was happening, had followed him out to the yard and checked to see that he was all right and able to continue playing. He was, after cleaning himself up and receiving a look of disgust from the owner of Birdland, Oscar Goldstein. Davis speculated that part of Jackie's problem was drug addiction because the young man had become a heroin addict when still very young.

'It came on the scene like a tidal wave,' Jackie explained, years later. 'I mean it just appeared after World War Two some kind of way.' He claimed that he and his fellow victims did not know, they just did not understand what they were getting into; they were targeted by the drug barons and pushers of the time, much in the same way that young people are targeted today; the drug barons have become greedier and greedier, ever pushing for larger communities of vulnerable victims and feeding on their ignorance and weakness.

McLean was honest enough, though, to point out that part of his own reason for experimenting with the drug was because his hero Charlie Parker was an addict. He also pointed out that almost all the young musicians of the day idolised Parker and thought that if he played better when he was high so could they. McLean was, by his own admission, to endure fourteen years of struggling to make a living and support a family – his wife Dollie, two sons and a daughter – while having an addiction to heroin. Somehow he managed to play the music he loved and support everything, including his habit.

Jackie had met Clarice Simmons, known to her friends as 'Dollie' at a party in the Bronx. She belonged to a strict West Indian family and unlike other women of Jackie's acquaintance she knew nothing about the jazz life or jazz musicians generally. They married in 1954 and Jackie assumed responsibility for her two young children from a previous marriage.[3]

One constant that stays with McLean all through the early years of his studies as a saxophonist and through his first years as a professional musician from around 1949 until 1955, is his relationship with Charlie Parker. Seen in perspective and up close, this can only be considered as both a blessing and a curse. But his admiration for the older man and Parker's somehow instinctive, intuitive realisation that Jackie was to be a major figure in the jazz of the future, drew them together and made them forever watchful of each other's progress.

There were often occasions when relations were strained between the two men, usually because of Parker's pawning of instruments when he was broke and desperate for yet another 'fix'. Sometimes it was Jackie's horn that Parker pawned, sometimes it was an instrument that the two musicians had rented between them, but the number of times it happened riled McLean. Parker, often broke or in debt, rarely had a horn in his possession and borrowing Jackie's was probably an everyday occurrence unless they rented. And there were many times when Parker used McLean's horn but did not return it and the instrument ended up lost or stolen. Mostly though, Jackie seemed to bend over backwards to forgive Parker or at least to see only the good in him.

'He was always trying to look out for younger musicians,' McLean recalled years later. 'At least that's the way I felt, you know.'

Parker also excelled in borrowing or extracting money from young McLean, sometimes taking it out of his pocket. He would ask Jackie how much money he had and how much he needed and ask him for the rest after McLean had stated a low figure. On some occasions, he put money back and even put back a lot more than he had taken, as Jackie recalled years later.[4] Although there were very many times that rented horns found their way into pawn shops, when he had money Parker would redeem them himself. It was the other times that Jackie found difficult.

The relationship between the two men had progressed from one in which Jackie was an admiring fan, a hero worshipper who had been flattered and delighted to be invited to sit in for the great man at a gig, to that of two musicians who often heard each other play and started to hang out together. But Jackie had seen several sides to Parker in those years, the older man a chameleon who changed colours from kind, thoughtful friend and mentor to heroin-addicted hard-case who would, in his colleague Dizzy Gillespie's words, 'sell his grandmother for a fix'. Parker at his worst was someone that even his closest friends kept their distance from.

A few days after an incident in NYC, when he showed his annoyance at Bird for losing yet another horn, Jackie read that Charlie Parker was dead. He was devastated and filled with remorse because he had snubbed Parker the very last time he had seen him, something that would leave a scar for many years after the event. Like all the modern jazz musicians he felt the loss deeply but, unlike many of the others, he had enjoyed a special relationship with the great alto saxophonist. He could not have realised it then but at that moment, the moment of Parker's death, he came out from under the giant shadow of Bird's all-embracing influence and began to develop as a soloist in his own right.

It was 1955, his playing was becoming ever stronger and ever more distinctive and he was on the threshold of a career that sent into reverse the usual jazz icon story: learn to play, play brilliantly, become famous, become addicted and die ridiculously young of drink, addiction and dissipation. Jackie got into the addiction very early in his life, began to play brilliantly, then became famous and multi-talented and turned into a respected educator. In 1955 he was poised, a little unsure of his direction but confident in the harsh environment of the recording studio and standing precipitously on that threshold.

4

STARTING AS HE MEANT TO GO ON

The more mature, confident alto saxophonist that Jackie McLean became began to make his mark and get himself noticed as early as 1955. He was twenty-four years old and beginning to get a reasonable number of gigs and to have recording opportunities. His development was fairly brisk and certainly impressive and by the time he went into the studios to record on two extended tracks on Miles Davis' *Sextet* LP of August 5th 1955 he was confident and self-assured. The two tracks, 'Minor March' and 'Dr. Jackle' were written by him and he takes the first solo on the former. Miles did not often use other soloists' compositions from within his own band or even outside it and when he did they were usually from seasoned contributors.

Jackie demonstrated his familiarity with, and ability to compose in, the standard bop language of the day. 'Dr. Jackle' is a rather complex line with, on this version, Milt Jackson on vibes leading the solo sequences, followed by Miles sounding calm, cool and collected. Jackie picks up the tag end of Miles' solo and is soon confidently spewing out hot flames of bop improvisation, double timing like a veteran and generally producing a lively and very impressive solo. The Parker mannerisms are still there to be sure and the phrasing is Parker bop too but McLean was building a professional solo style while openly admitting to taking a lot from Parker in his method of constructing solo lines. At this stage of his development he was well advanced as a modern soloist with the ability to construct solos at just about any tempo, play clean lines and ride on a good rhythm section. Individuality would come but it was not over-conspicuous in the August of 1955.

In October of that year he managed to get his first record date as leader of his own combo. The record was called *The New Tradition* and it appeared on a new but very short-lived label called Ad Lib (AD 6601). The sleevenote writer, Charlie Mack, referred to a new tradition of young musicians, particularly alto sax players, working in modern jazz and each being referred to as 'the new Charlie Parker'.[1] There was no new Parker, the writer asserted, but he went on to talk about McLean, his being influenced by Parker and the fact that Jackie acknowledged, in music and words, his relationship. So, although he was maturing rapidly and beginning to work out his own style and sound, complete escape from the giant shadow of Parker was not yet an option for him. Indeed he himself was happy to admit to using Bird licks frequently, feeling, rightly or wrongly, that they were the best, the ideal for the jazz of the day and that an aspiring jazz soloist should use them as required.

Mack also mentions Jackie's desire to give younger musicians a chance to play. He points out, rightly, that McLean could have chosen from the pick of seasoned NYC musicians to support him, but instead went for youngsters like himself whose experience was limited to say the least. Donald Byrd on trumpet was just a year older than Jackie and pianist Mal Waldron just a little older but hardly a household name at that time. Bassist Doug Watkins, just twenty-one, was beginning to be noticed as a member of the original Jazz Messengers but nowhere near as exalted a bass player as he later became. As for Ronald Tucker on drums, I have failed to find his name on any other record made before or since although he is reputed to have played behind Charlie Parker, Gene Ammons and Sonny Stitt in Philadelphia. And it should be noted that he plays very well in a post-bop, Blakey/Roach manner, lacking finesse perhaps but driving hard and assisting the achievement of swing. The only reference I could find to him outside this recording was by drummer Albert 'Tootie' Heath, who described him as 'a fine drummer from Philadelphia'. Mack could not have had any idea when he wrote his notes that promoting the careers of new musicians was to be almost a way of life for McLean, then and in the future, as he always sought to employ, promote and teach young players and help them to become established. Clearly his choice of personnel on his first quintet date indicated that he was behaving in the way that he meant to continue throughout his career.

The music on the record is bright, crackling hard bop, beginning on the opening track, 'It's You or No One' with a typically stark, attention grabbing opening solo by the leader, his sound open, almost acidic and riding on the pulsating rhythm section. The personal sound is beginning to shine through as early as this 1955 set, the tone a fascinating amalgam of Parker phrasing and the acerbic McLean sound that was so arresting and was to become his trademark. Jackie developed a strong blues approach from Parker, fastened almost exclusively on that aspect of Bird's playing initially, and slowly but surely began to fashion his own very personal sound in the years that followed. 'Blue Doll', written by Jackie for his wife, is an early example of his superior ability as a blues player although, on this version, the Parker mannerisms are perhaps a little too prominent. All the tracks here are worthy of close study and enjoyable even if much of the music leans heavily on earlier playing styles by Parker and Gillespie. And in 'Little Melonae', written for his young daughter, Jackie produced a strong line that became a modern jazz standard soon afterwards and was recorded by Miles Davis as well as many other leaders.

Incidentally as regards this early quintet recording, it was sold only in small numbers by Ad Lib, the company going out of business shortly after the disc was issued but it was subsequently reissued on the Jubilee label, JLP 1064. Consequently copies of Ad Lib 6601 in good condition are like gold dust and eagerly sought by collectors at auctions. The entire record, with all its faults, is an ideal introduction to early McLean and should be acquired by all enthusiasts interested in his early music.

On the club scene Jackie continued to play anywhere and with anyone to keep his chops in good shape and to continue learning his trade. Chances to play live as a leader were few and very far between although he grabbed whatever was offered with both hands. At one stage during the early days he had taken a very poorly paid gig as leader and, on advice from drummer Art Taylor, had offered Thelonious Monk a sideman job. Monk, who also was everywhere with everybody in those days, accepted and, according to Jackie, played contentedly all night and took his $12 sideman fee without comment and trotted off home.

By mid-1955, Jackie McLean, new leader on record, was working as a sideman in pianist George Wallington's sprightly bop quintet, along with Donald Byrd on trumpet, Art Taylor on drums and Paul Chambers on bass. On September 9th 1955, a month before the Ad Lib session was recorded, Jackie was working at the Café Bohemia in Greenwich Village with Wallington's combo and the band were recorded by Progressive Records, a small independent, live at the club. The Café Bohemia at this time was a major hot spot for jazz and jazz musicians. If they were not booked to play there they were frequently to be seen in the audience, sipping beers and nodding heads or being called up to the bandstand to sit in with the current combo. It was that sort of place. The owner had decided to initiate a jazz policy when Charlie Parker dropped in one day and suggested that it was a good room for music. Parker in fact was booked as the opening attraction and an advertising board was prepared with his name on it but sadly he died before he could fulfil the engagement. Perhaps it was fitting that the opening band that played in 1955 should feature the young man he had always encouraged, a musician who, at that time, came closest to reproducing the Parker style of bop.

Wallington was one of the first generation of boppers and had played piano in Dizzy Gillespie's band on 52nd Street at the start of the new music. Now he was something of a veteran at the age of thirty and leading a batch of bright youngsters in a hip NYC jazz club where everybody interested in the music went. The music played on that night was not the very greatest but it was a good sampling of bop played, at the age of around fifteen years, with relish, commitment and intensity by Jackie McLean and cohorts. Listen to the frantic opening and the tempo of 'Johnny One Note', and you may hear the beginnings of hard bop with Jackie playing in his facile, fiercely swinging Parker mode and upping the intensity levels before Byrd takes over on trumpet. Compare this to early 1940s examples of Parker and Gillespie and the intensity levels are very similar along with the basic, headlong bop stylings. The difference is heard in the gradual hardening up of the sounds, particularly McLean's alto. Jackie, already having acquired the nickname 'Jay Mac', as a selection on this disc by Byrd confirms, plays forcefully but in the language of the day. He is not, generally, as adventurous here as on his quintet date for Ad Lib but that is understandable. On that record he was promoting music written by himself or Mal Waldron, forging the beginnings of a personal style and backing the careers of four other young musicians; that session was bound to be more fresh and vital overall although the club date does have that electric 'live' club ambience.

Work was becoming plentiful: he had played many nights with Miles Davis and the Wallington engagement provided his first extended stay with a name band. He made the most of it, playing with strength and commitment, perhaps still leaning somewhat on the style of Charlie Parker. But with his penchant for playing just behind the beat, a tone that was developing into a highly charged, emotional cry at times and the percussive delivery that was becoming apparent on the 'Bohemia' engagement, he was beginning to sound distinctive. He was also consolidating his right to be taken seriously as a young, up-coming alto stylist. Wallington's combo at the Bohemia was followed there by the original Jazz Messengers with Horace Silver and Art Blakey in November and the first, great Miles Davis Quintet, with John Coltrane, Red Garland, Paul Chambers and Philly Joe Jones in 1956. In that year young McLean would make good progress and receive valuable advice from one of the master bass player/leaders in jazz.

5

ISN'T JACKIE McLEAN IN THERE SOMEWHERE?

1956 was a year of change and in many ways a new beginning for McLean. It began with a record date as leader for Prestige Records where he had signed an exclusive contract although, because of the company's methods, which included making only one take or winding back the tapes, not allowing paid rehearsals and discouraging original material, he would later regret the contract and complain bitterly about Prestige.

Lights Out (Prestige 7035) was recorded in Hackensack, New Jersey, on January 27th 1956. It begins with the title track, a long stretch of thirteen minutes, recorded with the lights out in the studio to provide the right late-night blues atmosphere for the musicians. Jackie takes a long, leisurely first solo, his agitated sound tracing his familiar blues-based bop phrases as he rides on the rock-steady rhythm provided by pianist Elmo Hope, bassist Doug Watkins and drummer Art Taylor. The Parker phrases are also applied quite liberally, as indeed they were on all his solos at this time – the fast runs and the blues inflections on virtually all material – but the alto was certainly starting to take on an unmistakable McLean sound that would soon become as instantly recognisable as that of the great Parker himself. Jackie's sound was percussive and with a cry of pain in it that made it distinctive.

Solos follow by Donald Byrd, muted, Elmo Hope and the entire quintet. The rest of the material follows the usual pattern at Prestige Records: blues lines, 'I Got Rhythm' variations and a standard, 'A Foggy Day'. As a result of Prestige allowing musicians no time to practise or prepare, all the material played at sessions like this had to follow the same method. Byrd's ballad 'Lorraine' is based on 'Embraceable You' and although it is the closest that inventive musicians could get to playing original material on Prestige record sessions, its 'parent' structure is immediately obvious.

Based mainly on variations of the blues, this is a popular early set by Jackie and a good indication of the way he sounded at the start of 1956. And the record sold well considering he was not a major name at that date.

Following work with George Wallington, Jackie accepted an offer to join the Charles Mingus Jazz Workshop and three days after the Prestige date in January 1956 he was in the studio again, this time to record as a sideman on *Pithecanthropus Erectus*[1] by the Mingus Workshop group. The title track, described by Mingus as a 'tone poem in four movements', is nearly eleven minutes long and is an advanced piece of jazz for its day, an early signpost for the free jazz movement of the 1960s. There are free passages in this piece which McLean contributes to as enthusiastically as anyone, indicating his willingness to embrace new ideas and experiment with sounds. Mingus' big-toned bass throbs around the edges of this composition for about five minutes and then the bassist begins to assert his authority on the direction the piece will take. Jackie's alto solo, following on from J. R. Monterose's tenor foray, is vivid, passionate and follows the direction Mingus intended with few Parkerisms to be heard. After relatively straight-ahead solos by tenor and alto there is a flourish of free jazz with everybody playing wildly and out of tempo. The first three movements are in ABAC form and the final one is based on the third but with an increased tempo. Although following a largely conventional tempo for much of the time the piece has the feel of later, free style jazz that came out in the early sixties after Ornette Coleman and Cecil Taylor had appeared on the scene. Mingus was, as usual, ahead of his time although his music was always more conventional in structure than that of the later 'free' players.

Mingus included 'A Portrait of Jackie' on this recording, a ballad written by the bassist for his young sideman where the altoist was the principal soloist. It is lyrical and richly melodic, quite a contrast from most of the rest of the material on this album. Again, early stirrings of a personal ballad style can be detected in Jackie's solo.

Charles Mingus was a larger than life figure, at one minute a towering, aggressive monster and a threat to anybody obstructing his path and the next a quiet, sensitive musician, fashioning a tender ballad on his bass or driving an excruciatingly intense uptempo jazz composition. Such a man was bound to be in conflict with many people around him but he was the leader who gave Jackie a lot to think about in the early years. Always original and inventive, Mingus' music was fresh, challenging, incomprehensible to some, the latest and the greatest to others, but one thing the bandleader could not abide was a musician who copied others and became a secondhand soloist. McLean claimed that it was Mingus who separated him from Parker and showed him that he had his own sound. In the liner notes to *Dynasty*,[2] Jackie's 1988 Triloka record, Will Thornbury quotes him as saying: 'I was in such awe of Bud, Dizzy and Monk...that as far as the saxophone was concerned, I was content to play what Bird played, or try to.' But Mingus said: 'Man, why do you keep on playing those Bird things? Isn't Jackie McLean in there somewhere? Bird already played that, man. Bird's dead now.' At first this was all far too heavy for the young Jackie who idolised Parker and resented Mingus for leaning so heavily on him. But, as McLean put it, 'Mingus stayed on top of me.'

'He'd write tunes that had no chords and no keys,' Jackie told Thornbury in 1995. 'I'd say, "What key are you in?" He'd say, "All keys are right." I'd say, "What about the chords?" No chords.... He helped me. I found Jackie during that period.'[3]

All this was, of course, invaluable training for Jackie's excursions into free jazz starting in 1962 but he couldn't have known anything about that at the time. The big benefit was finally getting him to release himself from the burden of being locked into the Charlie Parker method of alto sax solo playing. With his own rather tart alto sound consolidating into personal statements, and a manner of playing that put strong emphasis on the blues, he was still working on and developing over a relatively short period of time a slightly sharp, unique trademark sound. That came more and more into prominence with each gig and each new recording session.

Life with Mingus, ever problematic, was about to explode when the band went on tour and played a gig in Cleveland, Ohio. Mingus began berating Jackie on the stand and kept haranguing him repeatedly, all through the gig. Now, most bandleaders, if they had a problem with a sideman, would take him aside after the show and take issue with whatever he was doing wrong, in private. Not Mingus. He would blow up in front of an audience. Sometimes, indeed, he would harangue the audience for being too noisy and not concentrating on the music. It was all too much for McLean who came offstage and told Mingus that he was giving him two weeks notice. This led to a dreadful altercation where Mingus punched him in the mouth knocking back his two front teeth. The altoist, in a rage by now, attacked Mingus with a knife but somebody hit him on the arm and the bass player received only a minor cut. 'I'm so thankful of that,' Jackie told Thornbury many years later, referring to the fact that the knock to his arm prevented a serious injury or worse to Mingus.[4]

The leader sacked Jackie on the spot and left him stranded in Cleveland, without enough money to get back to New York. He had to pawn his saxophone to raise funds. Jackie also told

Thornbury that the American Federation of Musicians wanted to press charges against Mingus and throw him out of the union but McLean wouldn't agree to give evidence against him.

It might be thought that the association between the two men would end permanently at that point, but no. A year later Mingus invited Jackie to go up to Birdland and sit in with his band. Dollie McLean thought he was mad when he accepted and played tenor sax in the band. Backstage at Birdland Mingus hugged Jackie and showed him the little scar where he had cut him and said 'you tried to kill me.' Then he invited Jackie to rejoin his band on a tour that was coming up. On the way home from Birdland, in their car, Dollie said 'I know you're not even considering it.' Jackie smiled and replied, 'I am considering it,' and he ended up staying with the Mingus combo for another period of four months.

It was drummer Art Blakey who finally prised Jackie away from Mingus for good when he approached him after a gig and reprimanded him for working with the bassist. As Jackie related to Thornbury years later, Blakey asked him what he was doing in Mingus' band. 'That man hit you in the mouth! You ought to come with me.' It was a tempting offer. Blakey was going to Pittsburgh with a band that included pianist Kenny Drew and bassist Watkins who were, along with the drummer, among the best rhythm section musicians on the scene at that time. He also offered to buy a new alto saxophone for McLean who had been using a horn that belonged to Mingus and didn't own one of his own.

To avoid complications a certain amount of subterfuge was required. Blakey called for him the next morning, took him to town, bought him a horn, and then the two men took off for Pittsburgh without a word to Mingus. Mingus, in a rage, went round to Jackie's house and banged on the door, causing Dollie to threaten to call the police if he didn't go away. She told him repeatedly that Jackie wasn't in and Mingus repeatedly yelled that he knew he was. Later he sent Jackie a telegram telling him that he was going to dump him in the East River.

'That's how I left Mingus and ran away with Art,' Jackie said to Thornbury.5

Working with Blakey's Jazz Messengers enabled Jackie to blossom as a first rate young hard bop saxophonist. The band that was to run for several decades and become a virtual university of jazz playing was, in 1956, a fairly new outfit and only the second edition of the group. The first and arguably the very best edition of the Messengers had been a co-operative unit with Kenny Dorham, Hank Mobley, Horace Silver, Doug Watkins and the drummer, but Blakey began to take control early on, made all the announcements at concerts and, when the original combo split up, formed a new Jazz Messengers band where he was the undisputed leader. The band Art took to Chicago with Drew and Watkins was probably a pick-up group for a few gigs but, soon afterwards, Jackie found himself playing alto sax in the new Messengers with Bill Hardman on trumpet, Spanky DeBrest on bass and pianist Sam Dockery. He would record and play with them several times during that year but one disc stands out. Called simply *Hard Bop* it was virtually a blueprint for the new bop variation of that name. Everything that was good about the new hard bop style coalesced on that LP to produce a burning, churning, fresh sound of modern jazz that rang out the changes, literally and in every other way, to announce that a new, direct, emotion-charged style had been born and this was the way to play it.

The difference between bop as the pioneers had played it and the hard bop that was developed by people like Art Blakey, Max Roach and many others was that the music was stripped down to essentials. A hard, crisp but always flowing beat was allied to direct, emotionally forceful solos in the bop manner. Written themes became very brief and sketchy, intended as launching pads for the fast paced solos, and even ballads were approached in a muscular style. Sentimentality was out and spontaneous improvisation was in. There was no padding or filler material, the music was straight in the listener's face, strong and powerful. But it could, because of the solos, be very lyrical in a rather fierce manner.

As if seeking to tie McLean ever longer, ever more precipitously to the ghost of Charlie Parker and his style, the sleevenotes to *Hard Bop* by Nat Hentoff emphasize the great debt that this music had to Parker and his innovations. Later, in the same notes, Hentoff quotes from an interview in which Art Blakey talks about a visit he made to Parker on the day he died. Blakey claimed that Parker, answering a question about his best ever record, said 'I haven't made it yet,' and complained that young musicians of the day had forgotten their roots and were ignoring the most basic jazz ingredient: the blues.

Hard Bop goes back to the blues and back to basics in no uncertain manner. The music is explosive, blazing out with power and an emotive force from the soloists, particularly McLean, that is at times almost overwhelming. Blakey, who at that time was working out new methods of bringing the rhythm section into prominence, produced a style where the drummer was frequently as prominent as the front-line soloist. Although he had begun life as a swing drummer and retained many of the attributes of that style of playing, his press rolls, fills and generally commanding, booting style of drumming changed the way rhythm sections worked from around 1956 onwards. On this session he provides stimulating rhythmic support that at times is quite light and smoothly propulsive but, at other times, drives the soloist forward relentlessly with a barrage of accompanying bursts on his kit.

The record has fierce, passionate but lyrical readings of 'Stella by Starlight', Jackie's composition for his then two-year-old daughter 'Little Melonae', and a collaboration between him and trumpeter Hardman to produce 'Stanley's Stiff Chickens'. These give a good sampling of McLean's new approach to his instrument and his embracing of the hard bop style. 'Stella by Starlight', a popular standard, is here treated to searing, frantic alto sax solos and a multi-noted effort from the trumpeter. This is the new jazz, as it would have been heard by listeners in 1956 and an indicator of what was to come. Not many groups played with the commitment and intensity of Blakey's, and this record is one of his best, but it is historically overshadowed by a record by a new band in 1958 featuring their hit 'Moanin''[6] and consequently not listened to today as much as it should be. *Hard Bop* was good jazz and a statement of intent by the young boppers of 1956.

6

THE JAZZ LIFE

The jazz life has never been easy but it is a lot easier now than it was in 1956–57. Better music education in schools and colleges has helped, along with a much wider range of music for the professional musician to play, and the great growth of television, DVD, video and many other outlets. In Jackie McLean's early days on the road it was tough, with the drug culture still providing a harrowing backdrop to many musicians' lives. And if a musician was a known addict his cabaret card was taken from him, effectively stopping him from working in New York City clubs where most of the work was. It was a curious, if not heartless way, to treat somebody addicted but it was rigorously enforced in the 1950s.

Jackie in 1956 was a heroin addict with a family then consisting of his wife, daughter Melonae and son Rene, with another son on the way. Plus, of course, Dollie's two children from a previous marriage. As he said, the heroin thing swept in like a tidal wave and many musicians were caught up in it, particularly those, like McLean, who were heavily influenced by Charlie Parker.

Few if any people can envy the jazz musician's life: the unsocial hours, the scuffling for every gig and record date, the prospect of having to stand up in front of an audience, night after night, and virtually compose on the spot. And that with no chance of altering or recovering a wrong note once it has been played. They all knew that they had to practise hard because the music is not easy. As Jackie told Ken Burns in 1996. 'You had to have great speed…good energy…and a good knowledge of chord progressions and theory in order to play this music.'[1]

He went on to say that, in what he described as 'the University of Miles Davis', he learned how to study hard and play progressions; he also learned to play the piano and became efficient playing standards, something that he had avoided for a long time. Miles Davis was a good teacher but, like Mingus, a hard taskmaster and he made it clear to Jackie that he would have to put a lot of work into correcting the things he was weak on and not to rely on playing by ear to get himself out of trouble on gigs.

By mid-1956 and throughout 1957 Jackie had more or less conquered all his musical demons and was a first rate bop soloist, a man who could play the blues, standards, ballads and virtually anything else the hard bop jazz scene threw at him. Unlike many other jazz musicians he was able, miraculously considering the odds against, to keep working regularly.

The University of Miles Davis had done its job very well by late 1956. If McLean had been lazy and reluctant to learn to play standards in 1951–55, he was sounding like a master ballad player by the time he recorded *A Long Drink of the Blues* in two sessions in 1957 (Prestige New Jazz 8253). The title track features two long takes of a sturdy, slow blues where the leader and all his front-line soloists get to blow forcefully and at length. It's a good session but the reverse side of this LP, when it first appeared, featured three exceptionally well-performed standards recorded earlier the same year: 'Embraceable You', 'I Cover the Waterfront' and 'These Foolish Things', where he is backed by his old pal Mal Waldron at the piano, Arthur Phipps on bass and Art Taylor on drums. Jackie's tone, deep blue and threaded with melancholy, carefully constructs some of the most arresting and vibrant solos of his career to date. There is no longer the slightest doubt that he has learned his craft with regard to standard and ballad playing and learned it extremely well. The pain and suggestion of suffering and deep sadness that formed a feature of his solo work from this point onwards and even, occasionally, before, is present in abundance on these three sterling selections. Somehow, the skilfully played melodies are considerably enhanced by this feeling in his sound. Nobody in jazz exploited a natural ability to play the blues more convincingly than McLean at his best. And the blues are ever present on these performances even though none of the three is a blues composition.

There are plenty of examples of his work recorded at this time, most of them good or very good, and even those few that were slightly below standard seemed to benefit from his forthright, acerbic alto stylings. One or two that stood out did so, perhaps, because of the quality of the accompanying group. A two trumpet session with Donald Byrd and Art Farmer worked well on a Prestige disc of August 3rd 1956: *Two Trumpets* (Prestige PRLP 7062). Support from Barry Harris on piano, Doug Watkins on bass and Art Taylor, drums, could only enhance the quality of the recorded music. Harris and Watkins were among the many great rhythm sections that came from Detroit and seemed to suit Jackie for much of the early part of his career. Indeed the solid support given by Doug Watkins on bass began on Jackie's very first leader LP and continued until the bassist was tragically killed in a road accident in 1962 while travelling overnight from NYC to California to join Philly Joe Jones in a new trio he was forming.

Another session that worked very well, again with a trumpet player in a prominent, co-leader role, was *Jackie's Pal* (Prestige PRLP 7068). The co-leading 'pal' was Bill Hardman, the new trumpet player in Art Blakey's Jazz Messengers; the two musicians got on very well together musically and as friends when not in the recording studio. Again a first class rhythm section helps considerably and Mal Waldron, Paul Chambers and Philly Joe Jones were just the right musicians for the job.

McLean's Scene (Prestige NJLP 8212) was recorded partly at the end of 1956 with three additional tracks from February 1957.

This record provides a good example of how Jackie had matured and mastered some of the difficult areas that he appeared too lazy to deal with in 1954–55 when he was sometimes wary or at least uncomfortable with ultra fast tempi. Just listen to 'Outburst' where he roars along, taking the fast line by the scruff of its neck and meeting the challenge with ease. On the same disc he tackles the ballad 'Old Folks' and the sound of the alto is bittersweet, carrying a nostalgic edge from beginning to end. He has obviously, by this date, become highly proficient in the areas where he was most vulnerable.

The tone that McLean was developing at this time was hard, slightly acerbic but full of passion, almost wayward at times but adding up to a fascinating and deeply moving jazz sound. He was often criticised in the jazz press for what many perceived as the lack of control in his impassioned sound but, although sailing dangerously close to chaos at times, he was, I believe, ultimately always in control.

There was, however, a caring, highly emotional side to his personality, as shown through his home life and his concern for friends. He was, around this time, following the progress of his hero, tenor maestro Lester Young. Later he frequently used to visit the hotel room in New York City where Lester would sit and look across the road at Birdland, the club named after Charlie Parker, and watch the people coming and going. 'It was kind of sad,' Jackie related. 'He was kind of withdrawn.' He went on to say that Young would spend a lot of time sitting in his robe and pyjamas, drinking gin, staring out of his window or listening to vocal records on his gramophone. He would listen to Sinatra, Judy Garland or Billie Holiday records but never his own. 'And I would go to the store for him and get some gin or something, whatever he wanted...you know,' Jackie told Ken Burns.[2]

So how did someone so sensitive and caring for others come to play such aggressive music, his tone so frequently sounding angry? I believe it was a defence mechanism because he was hurting inside and the music was a way of letting off steam. His real feelings came out in the warmth and passion that every note of his music conveyed, no matter how slow or fast or whatever tempo was employed.

The other consideration was, of course, the period he lived through in the 1940s, '50s and '60s. Jackie said that he always felt that the world around the musician has a great influence on what he produces musically. 'You know, the propeller plane developed into the jet plane, and of course the atomic bomb and everything sped up,' Jackie said, 'and so did the music. The music began to accelerate.'[3] McLean was a musician of his time, picking up his general direction from first Lester Young and Dexter Gordon and then, a more shattering experience, the headlong originality and freshness of Parker, as he must have heard it and as it must have sounded to a young musician round about 1942 or 1943.

Throughout 1956 and 1957, Jackie recorded prolifically, mainly but not exclusively for Prestige. That company was one of the leading independent record companies producing modern jazz and the altoist fitted in very well with the music they were issuing at that time. Not only was he recording regularly as a leader but his services as a sideman were gratefully received by others such as trumpeter Donald Byrd, saxophonists Gene Ammons and Hank Mobley and several others. McLean, along with Cannonball Adderley and Phil Woods, was becoming one of the leading modern jazz alto players of the late 1950s.

Jackie was in and out of Blakey's Messengers at this time, as he tried, often unsuccessfully, to set up his own regularly working combo. Later in 1957 he formed a quartet with Gil Coggins on piano, bassist George Tucker and Larry Ritchie at the drums. The quartet eventually obtained a steady gig at the Club Continental in Brooklyn and after a time the leader was able to bring in Webster Young on trumpet or cornet; the two men had been gigging together for some time. Sixteen-year-old tuba player Ray Draper began to sit in with the band at weekends; during the week he was still at school. It was another example in the early days of Jackie helping and encouraging a young musician, this time with an unusual instrument for jazz.

The combination of alto sax, cornet and tuba gave a rare and fresh sound to the sextet and McLean managed to book the larger group into both the Club Continental and also a club in Sugar Hill, his old stomping ground and home turf. Fortunately this relatively short-lived band was recorded on a small, independent label called Jubilee: *Jackie McLean Plays Fat Jazz* (Jubilee JLP 1093) and it is well worth acquiring. Like many of the best but somewhat obscure jazz discs of the past it is not easy to find but it can be traced on Japanese CD or, more recently, Lonehill Jazz (LHJ 10269), where it shares space with Jackie's first record as a leader, the 1955 Ad Lib quintet session with Donald Byrd. 'Filide', the first track, shows up the fascinating blend of alto, cornet and tuba to advantage and gives us an idea of how exciting this band would have been when heard live at a 1950s jazz club. Jackie's alto solo flows along engagingly, buoyed up by Tucker's thick bass lines and Ritchie's vibrant cymbal beat. This joint composition by McLean and Ray Draper also features a ponderous but throbbing tuba solo that adds colour to the proceedings and, despite the instrument's cumbersome appearance, swings. This record is valuable for the writing for the three front-line instruments – the alto, tuba and cornet solos – and the indications of the way Jackie's group sounded in mid- to late 1957. 'Millie's Pad', a slow-burning blues, has that dark, blue-grey tone from Jackie's horn that pierces the air and produces a bitter sweet, melancholy sound.

The original liner notes to Jubilee 1093 by Jack Travis indicate that the band did not last long due to the economics of the jazz business (then as now) and suggest that club owners preferred small groups. The band might have survived a lot longer as a quartet but Jackie, typically, wanted to encourage young musicians like Webster and Draper and tried to keep the combo going with them in it, albeit only at weekends in Draper's case. So McLean headed back to the security of the Jazz Messengers and played some searing solos with them under Blakey's ebullient, charismatic leadership. Jackie said that Blakey was the best bandleader that he ever worked with and the two got on very well together during the years when the saxophonist was in and out of the Messengers. But that didn't stop Blakey inviting other young sax players onto the stand to play. 'And that was to keep me on notice,' Jackie told Ken Burns, 'that there was always somebody waiting in the wings.'[2]

Blakey would visit Jackie's house at this time and chat with Dollie and the children: Melonae, Rene and Vernon. Blakey, like McLean, put great stress on looking after his family. Both men were heroin addicts who managed, unlike most others, to control their addictions and lead relatively normal lives. And both were recording prolifically, together and apart, ensuring that steady income was obtained from records as well as whatever live gigs could be secured.

7

THE SHAPING OF A MAJOR SOLOIST

After the initial, almost overwhelming influence of Charlie Parker, the other people who helped to shape McLean's approach to jazz solos, playing and bandleading generally, were Miles Davis, Charles Mingus and Art Blakey. Jackie played with Miles in the early 1950s and the two became friends, riding the subways together, getting high and poking fun at the people they saw on the streets and in trains. It was juvenile behaviour, the high spirits of two young musicians who were often strung out and shared a similar sense of humour. But the music was always a very serious proposition for Miles, as it became for McLean, and the trumpeter was quick to criticize the young saxophonist if he did not perform on the bandstand. He discouraged him from taking the easy route and sticking to material he knew well at the expense of standards, ballads and new but difficult compositions. Miles made him think about the outcome if he did not learn to play popular material and berated him constantly to study and read the dots rather than rely on 'a good ear'.

Miles told Jackie that if he really wanted to get the feel of the music, he should stand next to the drummer. And so he used to stand to the right of Art's drum set and began to understand what Miles meant. Jackie said years later that he could feel the rhythm anywhere on the bandstand "'cause Art was so strong, and his style was about energy and thunder, you know, Art Blakey thunder."[1]

After learning the trick from Davis, Jackie would always stand next to the drummer at live performances and he claimed that his left ear was a little weak from listening to Art Blakey. In their prime, drummers Philly Joe and Elvin Jones were cited as the loudest on the planet by many commentators but musicians I have spoken to, who worked with all three, claimed that Blakey was the loudest of them all on occasion.

Blakey was, in McLean's opinion, the best bandleader he ever worked with and someone he liked, respected and admired. Apart from anything else he would have learned a lot from Blakey about the art of bandleading and getting on with the musicians he employed. Jackie claimed that he also learned about how to grow up and be a man because, 'Art was a very powerful individual that had things set in his mind, had a particular philosophy for having a band and everybody had to do their job or you were replaced.' In this respect Jackie recollected a night on the road with the Messengers in Philadelphia where Art invited a trumpet player up to the bandstand to sit in. McLean and Donald Byrd remembered a precocious young musician who came up and blew up a storm and occasionally would look across at the two front liners and wink at them. His name was Lee Morgan. Jackie pointed out that Morgan was making a joke of it and he was only sixteen at the time but he got the message. 'Donald was a master at that point,' Jackie recalled, 'and Lee was quite young, but he sounded very good, and so there was somebody waiting in the wings. So Art always had this thing going, you know.'[2]

In the liner notes to *Mirage*, the 1957 Jazz Messengers LP on Savoy MG 12171, Jackie enthused to annotator Burt Korall about Blakey, singing his praises and then added: 'He's strong, tenderhearted, firm and quite intelligent. He sets a pace as far as swinging goes, and few can keep up with him night after night.' Jackie McLean, by mid-1957, was one of the few that could and, overall, working with Blakey on a considerable number of occasions was probably the very best training he could possibly have had in those early years.

If Miles had been firm, and Blakey offered a number of solutions to a gifted sideman's problems, the time spent with Charles Mingus was the most traumatic but, overall, the most important of all lessons. Although with McLean's gifts he would surely have got there on his own, Mingus' repeated entreaties to play his own music and find his own voice were invaluable, and doubtless speeded up the learning process by a number of months and perhaps even years. 'Charlie Mingus was the most difficult bandleader I ever worked with,' Jackie said in 1996, 'because he was demanding, demanding rehearsal time, all the time.'[3] Mingus insisted that his band members rehearse at his house for hours, every day for weeks on end. It was a punishing schedule considering the long hours also spent playing engagements and, when the group was not working, Mingus called still more rehearsals.

The music played at that time was very demanding too, as Jackie said in 1996. Not for nothing did Mingus call his band the Jazz Workshop. If a selection did not suit the leader's requirements they would have to play it again, and again, and again. Sometimes the Mingus band would play the same composition over and over, all night long, in front of a long-suffering audience. And if anybody in that audience spoke too loudly they would receive an instant reprimand from Mingus and a demand to cut out the talking. McLean said he had seen Mingus pick up an exceptionally noisy member of the public and escort him to the door and physically throw him out of the club. 'Now that's the kind of guy he was,' Jackie said. 'He was a very powerful man and nobody wanted to get into any dispute with him because he had a short temper and seemed always ready for a fight.'[4]

Jackie recalled many bizarre moments while he was member of that Jazz Workshop. In Pittsburgh on one occasion Mingus had called for 'Pithecanthropus Erectus' repeatedly, in front of the audiences for two consecutive nights, with nothing else on the programme. Sometimes abruptly he would call a series of new tunes and carry on in more normal mode. McLean did not find any of this easy, as he has made clear in several different interviews, but he persisted, serving two periods of playing in the bassist's band and even returning again in 1959 for an Atlantic recording date (*Blues & Roots*: Atlantic 1305).

At rehearsals, Mingus would gather his musicians in one room and call each one to the piano in turn to go over their individual parts. He would, according to McLean, play, sing and teach the musician his part at the piano so that they would learn it and be able to play it, spontaneously on stage, with no music stands in front of them. Mingus hated to see sheet music on the stage. Jackie described how Mingus would take trumpeter Bill Hardman to the piano and teach him his part, and 'then he would call me over.' The musicians had to pick out their parts individually at the piano, then Mingus would call over the trumpeter and they would play both parts, then he would call the pianist, and they would finally rehearse the new music with the entire combo and no written music would go onto the stage.

A traumatic time indeed for any good professional musician but one where McLean admitted freely that he learned a great deal. Although he claimed to have been resentful and deeply offended by Mingus' constant entreaties not to play Bird licks, he did feel grateful to Mingus in the long haul. He said that Mingus helped 'me to discover myself, and to become more concerned with being original' instead of trying to be 'just another carbon copy' of someone he loved so much, like Parker.[5]

And that last lesson, for a soloist with considerable technical ability developing, was just about the most valuable of all that he learned in the early days.

* * *

1958 turned out to be relatively quiet for the saxophonist compared to the feverish recording and live appearance activities of

1956 and 1957. This may have had something to do with lacking a cabaret card and not being in the NYC clubs but Jackie only appeared on two LPs in 1958, and on both of these as a sideman. The recordings were for Blue Note, the top label of independent modern jazz records run by two keen enthusiasts, German immigrants, Alfred Lion and Francis Wolff. Unlike all the other independents, they provided several days paid rehearsal prior to the recording session and, on that day, filled the studio with good snack-type food and drink for the musicians to indulge in during the hours of recording. Bassist Bob Cranshaw has said that the only thing you had to do was swing, or, as Lion put it in his broken English, 'Swing, it must sving.' And Cranshaw added that you must finish. If there were eight tunes to record you had better play and record eight tunes before you could receive your cheque and head home.[6]

As a sideman, Jackie was always a major presence, sometimes even eclipsing the leader in the ferocity of his delivery and the invention in his solos. On a 1957 Gene Ammons date, *Funky* (Prestige PRLP 7083), he is at least the equal of the leader, the two men pouring out down-home blues choruses full of power and invention. Early in 1958, January 5th in fact, Jackie was recruited for Sonny Clark's *Cool Struttin'* on Blue Note 1588. One of the classic modern jazz dates on the label in what came to be known as the 'fifteen hundred series'. It is one of pianist Clark's very best sessions, for many people his masterwork, and it begins with the title track, a pulsating, medium tempo blues. Clark takes the first solo followed by a relaxed, laid back trumpet segment from Farmer. After this McLean's alto cuts through the air like a blue-bladed knife and reveals how much further his sound had developed into a personal voice. He was using spaces much more by this point, no longer piling notes on notes rapidly and indiscriminately – something else he had learned from Miles Davis.

Nat Hentoff's liner to this release quotes Art Farmer as saying, 'most of the altoists took one primary aspect from Bird – there were so many to the man – and developed that one for their own purpose. With Jackie he took that real agonised tone – sometimes it's like a squawk – that Bird would use at times. So Jackie developed on that and paid little attention to the more delicate elements of Bird's playing. Jackie has a feeling in his playing that you know immediately it's him. He doesn't just copy.' This was a very perceptive remark by Farmer, particularly as early as 1958, for although it is an over-simplification, it does indicate what Jackie had been doing in the late 1950s and the way his style was being developed. I personally think that McLean latched onto two aspects of Parker's style: his agonised tone, as Art called it, and a searing, blues sound that he managed to inject into everything he played, whether or not it was in a blues format. At any rate the *Cool Struttin'* session represented the latest, rapidly maturing McLean alto sound and, together with the considerable contributions of Clark, Farmer, Paul Chambers on bass and Philly Joe Jones on drums, produced one dynamite hard bop record. The initial four tracks recorded on that date were augmented on later CD issues with two more: 'Lover' and 'Royal Flush' which were scheduled for a second volume (Blue Note 1592) that was shelved by the company and never issued. It came out in the late 1970s on a Japanese Blue Note and is well worth acquiring by anybody who does not have the two extra, extended tracks.

On December 21st 1958 Jackie was back at Hackensack to take part in a recording for his old mate Donald Byrd (*Off to the Races*: Blue Note 4007) where once again his acidic but passionate alto can be heard to advantage. And that, for one reason or another, was the extent of his recorded work for that year. As he was unable to be engaged by NYC clubs, work was most likely sparse and would have involved trips to other parts of the country or abroad. It must have been a hard year.

8

BLUE NOTE BEGINNINGS

1959 was a crucial year in McLean's development as a major jazz soloist. He signed a contract with Blue Note Records and on 18th January he recorded the first three tracks of *Jackie's Bag* (BLP 4051), his first and one of his best LPs for that company. But, although the first three tracks were scorchers, everything they tried after that did not work out. The recordings were put on one side and did not get released until a year later when McLean had already put out three other discs on the label. On February 5th he went into the Atlantic studios to play as a sideman on *Blues and Roots*, another significant modern jazz recording, for leader Charles Mingus.

Jackie, like many others before him, had severe problems working for Mingus. Even so, differences were eventually ironed out and a state of equilibrium reached between the two men as Jackie went back for a third time to record with the bassist. The charismatic but volatile and highly unpredictable bandleader seemed to act like a magnet to McLean, drawing him in and extracting some of his finest solos at that time.

By the end of that year the first article about McLean appeared, not in one of the main jazz magazines on home ground, *Down Beat* or *Metronome*, but in a small, privately owned publication in Britain, run from a private house in St. Austell, Cornwall, called *Jazz Monthly*.[1] The author, Michael James, a British novelist and jazz journalist suggests that McLean 'never made the mistake of trying to assimilate the whole of the master's work; rather did he build assiduously on one of its more important aspects: the freedom of phrase in relation to the construction of the solo at large.' James goes on to suggest that it is noticeable that McLean's rhythmic approach is tied more rigidly to the mechanics of the beat than Parker's. Parker's rhythmic approach was far more fluid than that of anybody else playing jazz and when James suggests that the variety in Parker's work finds 'but a distant echo in the younger man's work', it is difficult to disagree. In any case, he adds that McLean's lines are just as irregular and suggests that his phrases have a personal lilt 'that runs counter to the basic movement only to enhance its strength'.

James refers to Jackie as an uncompromising soloist who makes no concessions to good taste in the form of evasion of less attractive moods. He feels that a sense of loss, frustration and even bitterness pervades McLean's work and notes that the sharp pitching, spare phrasing and strained enunciation combine to form an intense yet satisfying whole. Then he claims that on some occasions, 'the mass of feeling overflows into incoherence'. James says that McLean could still be baffled by a fast pace and suggests that listeners not willing to make a necessary, sympathetic effort will be repelled by the emotional aura. He also feels that the amount of playing the altoist did in the Blakey Messengers group was ideal as it forced McLean to play within the confines of a logical form. All of which is interesting and makes sense although it should be noted that the context in which James was writing at the time was considerably restricted. None of McLean's records made after February 1957 were available to the writer and consequently he was in no position to understand the advances Jackie's music had made in 1958 and 1959, or even the later 1957 recordings. James concludes by claiming that it would be wrong to present his subject as a revolutionary but says that he has developed one of the routes opened by Charlie Parker and, unlike Rollins, 'is relatively unconcerned with protracted form'. He sees McLean's work as having brought, 'probably unconsciously, a heroic touch to the music of his place and time'.

It is a strong, admirable tribute to a soloist who had, seemingly, not been noticed by anybody in his own country up to that date. There would be many, many more articles on Jackie McLean to follow in the years ahead but the very first came from a writer who was only in a position to cover the early and, for reasons stated above, immature soloist that McLean was up to 1957. In 1959 however came the first important turning point with the Blue Note recording contract and a play from the Living Theatre Company called *The Connection*.

* * *

As the first three tracks of *Jackie's Bag* lay collecting dust on the shelf, waiting for three new tracks to join them, the altoist went into the studio at Hackensack, New Jersey, on May 2nd 1959, to record *New Soil* (BLP 4013). With Donald Byrd on trumpet and what was probably close to his working band of the time: Walter Davis Jr. on piano, Paul Chambers on bass and Pete LaRoca on drums. This record shows how far McLean had developed since his first record dates with Davis, just over eight years earlier. The compositions on *New Soil* are well structured and not just loose blowing themes. The opening 'Hip Strut' is a slow, insistent theme that Jackie improvises on at length after sharing some loose counterpoint with Byrd on the opening ensemble.

'*New Soil* is my idea for a title,' Jackie told sleeve annotator Joe Goldberg. 'This is a change in my career. My style's changed, I've changed. I'm not like I used to be, so I play differently.' Using four compositions from his pianist, Walter Davis, and two of his own, the leader fashioned a diverse programme that included plenty of solo room for his sidemen. On 'Minor Apprehension', LaRoca takes a long, complex solo in which he plays 'impressions of the tune' according to his leader. Jackie's own solos contain fast bop licks and, on 'Hip Strut' and 'Greasy', slow, measured blues phrases with plenty of spaces between notes and examples of his mature alto playing which now has the sound of McLean first and foremost and only traces of the Parker style it was fashioned from. Jackie also points out in the sleevenotes that he spent five weeks producing and recording this album. 'There's a good band sound here,' he declares, 'because we had time to work things out. A lot of times, you go into the studio, play and walk out.' This, as he acknowledges, was because Blue Note allowed plenty of time for leaders to plan and rehearse and the results justified the extra costs that they must have paid out to achieve it. At Prestige it was just possible to work out no more than three or four standards and a blues on the spot, although it should be pointed out that those methods, very occasionally, produced startling, brilliant results: Sonny Rollins' 1956 session *Saxophone Colossus* springs immediately to mind.

There is a warmth along with a lyric beauty in many if not most of the selections in *New Soil* that justify the extra preparation and, with few exceptions, Jackie's Blue Note LPs represent the very best of his early music. This LP was the first to be heard due to the delays in putting out *Jackie's Bag* and it heralded the first of several 'new Jackie McLeans'. The writing played a fairly big part in the success of the album and, for this reason, Walter Davis deserves plaudits for his 'Davis Cup', 'Sweet Cakes', and rhythm and blues based 'Greasy', all of which offered something a little out of the ordinary at the time.

Joe Goldberg's sleevenote is also revelatory for the insight it offered into McLean's life at this time. Mentioning that he has a wife and three kids and saying that his eldest boy Rene is going to be a sax player, Jackie goes on to paint a brief but revealing portrait of his home life at the time. He says he used son Rene's sax on the date and then goes on to claim that he spends most of his time at home. 'I stay around the house mostly – playing chess – everybody in the house plays except my daughter

Melonae; you can always get a game – practising and writing. We just got a piano, and I'm learning to play so I can write on it.'

Family life was obviously very important to Jackie at this point as his comments to Goldberg made clear. Unlike his early hero Parker, who indulged in anything and everything and was often unreliable due to his drug addiction, McLean appears to have made his mind up from the very start that, come what may, he was going to fight for and maintain a happy home life, looking after the interests of his family and, very important this, when he was not actually out on the road playing, spend his time at home with them all. It couldn't have been easy, particularly considering that his cabaret card had been taken away and he was unable to perform in New York City clubs and bars. Live performances in clubs, the mainstay of all the best jazz soloists, would have meant frequent travels around the country and sometimes abroad and all these considerations would have put extra strain on his marriage and home life.

'I think I have my own style now, my own sound and my own approach,' Jackie told Goldberg in the spring of 1959. He had learned a lot from Miles Davis, particularly in regard to not playing a multitude of notes on every piece but only the necessary ones. In other words, using space intelligently, which McLean started to do more in the late 1950s.

On October 2nd, with the three tracks from *Jackie's Bag* still on the shelf, the altoist went into Rudy Van Gelder's studio to record *Swing Swang, Swingin'*, his next Blue Note LP. With a strong rhythm section comprising Walter Bishop Jr. on piano, the up-and-coming Jimmy Garrison on bass and the reliable Art Taylor at the drums, Jackie recorded a programme of six sturdy standards and a twelve bar blues, '116th and Lennox'. Miles Davis had made his point well: by this juncture McLean could run through hardy pieces like 'What's New', and 'I'll Take Romance' as though he had been playing them every night for years. 'What's New' is here taken at a slow to medium tempo and, although there is a strain of melancholy running through it, this is a highly personal and original version, showing him using space well and inventing lines around the basic melody with apparent ease. Compare this with Parker's version on Verve and it will soon be seen that McLean, vintage 1959, was now very much his own man and a significant soloist. There was a long way to go though and his home life was probably being threatened daily by his lack of club work in NYC. But at this point he managed to circumvent the problem by appearing onstage in the theatre as a musician and actor. He was about to make quite a mark in Jack Gelber's *The Connection*, a play about drug addiction.

9

THE CONNECTION

The irony would not have escaped McLean and his family on July 15th 1959 when the altoist began work as a musician and actor in Jack Gelber's highly controversial play *The Connection*. The Living Theatre in New York City presented the play about four jazz musician addicts waiting around in a seedy pad for their 'connection', a character called 'Cowboy', to arrive. The four actors are joined from time to time by a playwright, a producer and two photographers and a sort of play within a play takes place as these latter characters are supposedly shooting an avant-garde film of the play.

McLean, at this time addicted to heroin and not allowed to perform in jazz clubs in NYC, was allowed to appear on stage in a New York theatre, playing saxophone and acting and – yes, that's right – playing a jazz musician who is addicted to heroin. The music for the play had been designated by the writer Jack Gelber as being 'in the tradition of Charlie Parker'. By all accounts, Gelber would have been happy for the musicians on stage to play standards and various twelve bar blues concoctions but when pianist composer Freddie Redd was hired to lead the bop quartet on stage, he made it clear that he wanted to produce all new music, specially composed for the play. Gelber, who was very happy with this suggestion, promptly armed Redd with a script and that is how the music for *The Connection* was born.

McLean and Redd were old friends and had played together in clubs and concerts frequently. Although the rhythm section changed often in the first few months, it settled down when bassist Michael Mattos and drummer Larry Ritchie were recruited and they stayed, along with Jackie and Freddie, until the play ended its run. It is fascinating and instructive to go to *YouTube* on the internet and view the sample from the film of the play shown there. A slim, youthful-looking McLean can be seen and heard blowing alto in that emotive, blues inflected manner he had, with Redd pounding out the chords at the piano, and Mattos and Ritchie supporting on bass and drums. As the music plays, the action of the play, such as it is, continues. A photographer worries about running out of film for his avant-garde movie and various characters slouch around or sit looking vacantly into space, waiting hopefully for their fix to arrive. A second drummer, sticks in hand but with no kit, apes every movement Ritchie makes, flourishing the air with the drumsticks. After a minute of silence and little stage activity an actor urges Freddie to 'play something' and the pianist launches into a new composition.

The music written for the play, which includes 'Music Forever', 'Wiggin'' and 'Theme for Sister Salvation', is best heard on two discs first released in the early 1960s: *The Music from the Connection* by the Freddie Redd Quartet featuring Jackie McLean on Blue Note BST 84027, and an album featuring Redd, tenor saxist Tina Brooks (Jackie's understudy in NYC) and trumpeter Howard McGhee, reissued as Boplicity CDBOP 019. The play ran for more than three years and McLean was part of the company travelling to the UK in 1961. A production in California featured Dexter Gordon in the part Jackie played in NYC. Although harrowing as presented with all the realism that the actors and, particularly, the musician-actors could inject into it, the play was a success. It shocked and worried a lot of people in the 1960s, people who went regularly to the theatre but didn't expect, at that time, the levels of realism that were presented to them.

'No, it was like that,' Jackie said in 1994. 'It was like that was a real hunk of life, that play. It was way ahead of its time.'[1] He went on to add, chillingly, that America later experienced widely the problems the play had predicted. And he added, perhaps tellingly, that when the company arrived in Britain, the play didn't work very well because there was no drug problem in the UK at that time. 'They had legalized drugs over there,' he told the interviewer and went on to say that there was no waiting for a connection to arrive in Britain because addicts could get drugs from their doctor. 'They had three drug convictions in the whole country.' This statement prompts the obvious question, whatever happened to the enlightened attitude and laws of 1961?[2]

This was a successful period in McLean's early years as a professional jazz musician and he acquitted himself well as an actor. Much of the credit for the play's success, however, must go first to Gelber and then to Redd for his high quality music score and, of course, to the rest of the quartet that played it night after night.

Aficionados will hear some of McLean's best solos of the period on the Blue Note *Connection* disc, recorded in February 1960. He is both brash and at times acerbic and, as always, there is that distinctive undercurrent of melancholy as in all his work at this time. Given that this was a result of his lifestyle, my only surprise, if that's the right word, about *The Music from the Connection*, would be that it is almost all bright and upbeat. A couple of dark, sombre minor compositions would surely have suited the mood and ambiance of the play? Only Freddie Redd can address that comment but it must be acknowledged that all the music from the play is memorable, distinctive and, of course, enhanced considerably by the solos of McLean and Redd and the rhythm backings.

* * *

The changes in McLean's mature style began in 1959 and possibly much of it was worked out as he played, night after night, in *The Connection*, working on the same Freddie Redd compositions but doubtless applying fresh variations over a period of nearly three years. He was always a restless, explorative soloist and, unlike most, unwilling to set a style and play it virtually unchanged for the rest of his life. The new sound of McLean was to be heard late in 1959 and much more in 1960. Perhaps by coincidence, some of his most advanced and probing solo work was caught in January 1959 when he recorded 'Blues Inn', 'Fidel' and 'Quadrangle', for Blue Note. In 1960, three tracks from a September 1st session were added to make up *Jackie's Bag*, which came out later that year on Blue Note BLP 4051.

The first three pieces show how much Jackie's writing had developed and matured. 'Quadrangle' is a fascinating composition which he admitted in 1962 (in the notes to *Let Freedom Ring*) did not fit easily with rhythm changes. When these tracks were recorded, however, he was in the process of working out new methods of writing and playing and the style here is not much removed from earlier attempts in this type of piece. Even so, the alto solo is intense, supercharged and swings like mad, courtesy of Jackie's own inbuilt sense of time and the driving, slashing rhythm section comprising Sonny Clark, Paul Chambers and Philly Joe Jones, one of the best units he worked with. 'Quadrangle' benefits from exceptional solos by McLean and Philly Joe with Clark laying out on this track. Listen to the pianist on *Fidel* where he easily matches the invention and intensity of the leader. McLean stated in the liner notes to *Jackie's Bag* that he had written 'Quadrangle' four years earlier and it had been a style of writing he had been working towards for some time. 'I had some trouble at first putting chords on it for blowing on,' he continued, 'but I wanted to have a firm basis to play on, as well as those figures that came into my head.'

In the year and a half separating these two sessions, Jackie had begun playing modal music more frequently and had found other ways to interpret pieces like 'Quadrangle'. Playing on scales rather than the more conventional chord progressions was something that he had learned in Charles Mingus' Workshop bands in 1957 but it had not become common practice by 1960. Much of Mingus' practice at the time was forward looking and original but, as with all things, it took the general public and most other musicians, a long time to catch up. The main thrust of inspiration for Jackie is most likely to have been Miles Davis' groundbreaking Columbia LP *Kind of Blue,* recorded in March 1959 and beginning to gain momentum on its journey towards becoming the best-selling jazz record of all time. Davis, who pushed McLean to play standards and to study music thoroughly, also taught him to use space intelligently and effectively. So it should come as no real surprise that on the second session that made up the six tracks of *Jackie's Bag,* the altoist kicked off with 'Appointment in Ghana' which uses a modal structure in the main phrase. As Bob Blumenthal noted in his insert for the updated CD release of *Jackie's Bag* in 2002, the practice of playing scales had not entered McLean's writing until this session.[3] 'It provided an alternative to standard harmonic sequences that McLean would apply to later performances of 'Quadrangle', and that served him well in the more open approach he would soon document on such albums as *Let Freedom Ring* and *One Step Beyond.'*

All that was in the future; in 1959 and through most of 1960-62, Jackie was developing as a major soloist and experimenting with new forms and methods of expression. By the time *Jackie's Bag* was released in 1960, he had already put out three good Blue Note LPs including *New Soil* and *The Music from the Connection*. Over that period of time his music had begun to move very slowly away from the solid hard bop of 'Quadrangle' towards more modal and challenging writing and playing such as we find on the six 1960 tracks that comprise the full, 2002 release of *Jackie's Bag.* Over the next two years it would change even more radically and dramatically but on the later tracks of this album he shared composition duties with the brilliant, ill-fated tenor saxophonist Tina Brooks. It was Brooks who played tenor on these tracks and the blend of his gospel-influenced, warm tenor and Jackie's often strident, slightly sharp, bluesy alto sound was wonderfully successful. Also featuring Blue Mitchell on trumpet, Kenny Drew on piano, Art Taylor at the drums and Paul Chambers as bassist on both dates, these selections really smoke and pulsate with vibrant modern hard bop solos.

Jackie's Bag turns out to be one of Jackie's most successful Blue Note albums of all and the others were all in the very good category. Perhaps it was the fact that the first session had only produced three good tracks that made this, eventually, the big success story that it became. When the later six tracks were added it offered stirring music from some of the best front-line and rhythm section players active at the time and, duly inspired by all of them, some of the very best McLean solos available to that date.

During the early 1960s Jackie recorded prolifically for Blue Note and other companies and his records offer a selection of standard but very adventurous hard bop, but also new music that is experimental and searching. From around this time it should have been obvious that McLean was not a musician to be put into any single category although it is true that the man who had followed, played with and shared a horn on occasions with Charlie Parker never abadoned his lifelong love affair with bebop.

On April 17th 1960, he headed to New Jersey for the Englewood Cliffs studio of engineer Rudy Van Gelder to record *Capuchin Swing*, (Blue Note 84038), with Blue Mitchell, Walter Bishop Jr., Paul Chambers and Art Taylor in support. It is another first rate release with tracks such as 'Francisco' and 'Condition Blue' outstanding. More Blue Note recordings followed in 1961, an important year if only for the release of two really exceptional albums: *Bluesnik* recorded in January of that year and *A Fickle Sonance* recorded on October 26th.[4]

The end of that year saw two enthusiastic hard core followers of the musician, Dick Prendergast and Jim Harrison, staging a special concert, *An Evening with Jackie McLean*, at Judson Hall in NYC. These two, named by Ira Gitler in his sleevenotes to *Fickle Sonance*, had felt that the New York cabaret card restriction was grossly unfair and they staged this special event which included a table in the foyer displaying the covers of all the LPs featuring McLean as leader. Whether it had any effect on the NYC Police Department is unknown but surely unlikely. It does show however the extent to which fans of the saxophonist were willing to go and how much they felt that his banishment from New York clubs was unreasonable. It also demonstrated just how well-known and appreciated he had become in the lives of jazz enthusiasts who, even though they could only hear him at theatres, at least had a fair number of recorded performances to enjoy.

Jackie McLean had made it in terms of recognition as a major jazz soloist and bandleader.

10

BLUESNIK

In January 1961 when Jackie recorded *Bluesnik* for Blue Note Records he could hardly have been aware that he was producing one of his masterworks. It is perhaps somewhat ironic that one of his most basic and simple to construct record sessions should produce what is arguably his best ever single recording. The major musicians of the late 1950s and 1960s all seemed to come up with a definitive LP that encapsulated all that they had achieved up to that point: a summation of their art in music. Sonny Rollins produced *Saxophone Collossus* on Prestige, Coltrane came up with *Giant Step*s on Atlantic and Hank Mobley recorded *Soul Station*, some of the very best of the best in each case.

In the case of *Bluesnik*, Jackie wrote two numbers, pianist Kenny Drew contributed three and trumpeter Freddie Hubbard provided one, which together assembled a programme of six variations on the blues. The quintet also included Doug Watkins who had a great affinity with modern blues and was said to be the bassist of choice for Alfred Lion at Blue Note during those hectic years of recording contemporary jazz. Typically, Jackie chose the young drummer he had worked with several times, Pete LaRoca, although I suspect he could easily have lined up Philly Joe, Art Blakey or Art Taylor.

The most important jazz soloists have always been comfortable and steeped in the blues idiom: in Jackie's line of descent, Sonny Stitt, Charlie Parker and later Ornette Coleman. On this disc the leader starts off with 'Bluesnik', a fast, scorching blues where his alto stylings are constantly inspired and driven by

Watkins' sturdy bass line and LaRoca's ringing cymbals. The blues sound is raw and urgent, the cry in his tone piercing. This is blues alto playing of a very emotive hue. 'Goin' Way Blues' is, by contrast, slow and funky, a low down blues that allows McLean, Hubbard and Drew to fashion urgent, preaching solos. 'Drew's Blues', by the pianist, is a loping, fascinating piece which offers yet another variation on this form but still allows the soloists, notably Jackie and trumpeter Hubbard in this instance, to fashion biting, passionate solos. McLean's slurs and drawls add to the blues ambience and everybody plays with warmth and conviction.

'Cool Green' is an ultra cool minor blues that slouches along rather than skips, in true blue fashion. Jackie's solo is bleak and emotive here to a greater degree than some of his other solos but all these tracks coalesce together to make one of the best programmes of blues-infused hard bop ever put on record. 'Blues Function' by Freddie Hubbard is, indeed, a very functional blues line. This composition is the most typical of the twelve bar form but any impression of ordinariness the piece might contain is negated by the quality of the solos, first by a bright, brassy Hubbard, followed by an intense, preaching McLean.

The final track, 'Torchin'', is a medium tempo, laid-back blues which seems carefully constructed, both in the written line and the execution by the musicians. Jackie digs into his solo entrenched in blues licks and is followed by a jerky, jittery, staccato Hubbard, who makes a fascinating job of his lines on this track. Drew is fleet but effective. The track ends with what sleevenote annotator Ira Gitler describes as 'a pianistic amen' with Watkins' bow seconding Drew. The CD reissue of the album also includes an alternate take of this piece and a second version of 'Goin' Away Blues'.

The choice of personnel also helped to make *Bluesnik* the impressive, hard-swinging document that it was. The young, upcoming Hubbard with his clean lines and inventive turns of phrase was an ideal trumpet choice. What he lacked in experience at the time, he made up in enthusiasm and the freshness of his approach. Technically he was already well ahead of the field, even before his twentieth birthday. As well as Jackie, he played with Donald Byrd, Lee Morgan and Blue Mitchell, and familiarity might have bred a certain amount of – not contempt exactly – but merely going through the motions. For a brave project like this, presenting six variations on the blues, a programme that could have produced a lot of sameness of execution in the wrong hands, Jackie was well served by the ambitious, very keen to do well, Hubbard. Another excellent choice was Drew, a pianist who had the blues running through his veins, judging by the way he played. With the possible exception of Sonny Clark, Drew was the only pianist on the Blue Note roster at that time who could have contributed so well to the success of this record.

The bass duties could not have been in better hands. Doug Watkins was McLean's first choice for this assignment. He had engaged Watkins from his first date as a leader on Ad Lib in 1955, through most of his Prestige dates in 1955–58 and they had worked together on Donald Byrd's 1959 *Fuego* LP and on *Byrd in Flight* in 1960. This was the last occasion when the two friends recorded together.

Pete LaRoca Sims, to give him his full title, was in demand in the period from the end of the 1950s through the early years of the 1960s. He worked with Sonny Rollins, John Coltrane and many others and was beginning to make a name for himself as a swinger in top bop groups. For some reason he left music later in that decade and surfaced again after some thirty-five years and, at the time of writing, is still playing and recording.

Bluesnik, with or without the two alternate takes, is one of the most swinging, intense, emotive explorations of modern jazz derived from the blues and the variations in tempo and approach to the form will give any serious jazz enthusiast a very enjoyable listening experience. I should know, I bought my first mono LP copy over forty years ago and I've never tired of listening to it. A stereo LP and two CD copies later, it still represents one of my most frequent choices of disc to listen to and enjoy. If anybody wanted to buy one McLean record and only one, this is the one I would have to recommend.

11

NEW DIRECTIONS AND OLD STANDBYS

If *Bluesnik* is the most satisfying, completely realised recording that McLean made in the very early 1960s, it is only one of a series of striking, often surprising recordings from him in that decade. It was a time of change, a time of seeking, and frequently finding, new avenues and methods of expression. 'Getting away from the conventional and much overused chord changes was my personal dilemma,' he wrote on the *Let Freedom Ring* album liner in 1962 and he succeeded eventually after many new attempts to change the manner of his playing.

Bluesnik, brilliant though it is, remains a set of bop-based blues performances and a recording he made with Kenny Dorham in that same year is also in the tradition. *A Fickle Sonance*, recorded in October 1961, is a remarkable session that I suspect Jackie was not quite satisfied with. He later quoted 'A Fickle Sonance' as one of his compositions that he felt did not fit in with 'I Got Rhythm'-type changes in his improvised solos. He similarly stated in relation to 'Sonance' and 'Quadrangle' from his 1959 *Jackie's Bag* LP 'These changes do not fit the personality of the tune at all.' He made it clear that listening to Ornette Coleman had 'made me stop and think'.[1] But as Bob Blumenthal pointed out in the notes to the reissue of *A Fickle Sonance* in 2000, 'in this performance of 'A Fickle Sonance' it is also clear that the technique of improvising on modes that Miles Davis had popularized on *Kind of Blue* provided a more immediate solution to the lingering compositional problems.'

Once again, McLean was listening closely to Davis and taking ideas of form and expression from his friend. As British writer Michael James noted in 1958 when he corresponded with Jackie, 'Thelonious Monk and Miles Davis were the two musicians who were then having the greatest effect on his own style.' McLean told James that one of the chief facets of Davis' style was his ability to wring so considerable an impact out of an austere melodic line. James concluded that McLean was working towards a similar goal himself and this is borne out by the intensity and emotive force to be heard in Jackie's tone from 1959 onwards. It was Ira Gitler, in the original liner notes to the first issue of *Sonance*, who produced a phrase that is in my opinion the ultimate description of McLean's sound: 'Jackie's horn can cut a hole in your heart and let the night pour through.' I doubt if you'll ever find a better descriptive phrase than that to describe the effect of McLean's alto sound soaring into the air.

'Five Will Get You Ten' is the opening track on *Sonance* and one of those spiky, catchy, clever lines associated with Thelonious Monk. Not surprising really as it turns out that he wrote it and it was miscredited to Sonny Clark, pianist on the date, on the original LP issue. Clark had been hanging out at the home of Nica De Koenigswarter, the jazz baroness as she was known, and friend and supporter of Monk and Sonny. He had heard it there, liked it and taken it to the session. The music on *A Fickle Sonance* is varied but thoroughly refreshing and it does signal a new McLean in the making without being particularly radical or even different from the records he had made just a few months earlier. This is partly due to a new and stimulating rhythm section. Previous records had featured great rhythm players, many of them the best in the business at that time, but those musicians were thoroughly acquainted with his style and manner of expression so perhaps a little lethargy had crept into some of their work together. The section comprising Sonny Clark, bassist Butch Warren and drummer Billy Higgins was unique and special in its ability to provide fresh lines, a compulsive but relatively light swing and a contemporary sound that was based securely on the bop and hard bop styles of the past. Clark was a flowing pianist whose lines resembled those of Bud Powell without the nervousness and tenseness. Sonny just sounded so relaxed and his music flowed along like a river.

'Subdued' is, simply, the ideal slow, melancholy jazz ballad; the alto lines full of emotive yearning, the solo building slowly from the simple melody to a complete, complex statement of Jackie's art encapsulated in one six-minute performance. Trumpeter Tommy Turrentine's muted solo is tense and beautifully crafted but it is Clark's sympathetic accompaniment and flowing piano solo that truly enhance and make this track special. He injects real pathos into his solo segment, echoing brilliantly the leader's sombre reading. There is little doubt also that the freshness and talent of this rhythm section inspired Jackie to put one of his best performances on record. Turrentine too deserves praise for his sterling work as front-line partner to McLean. The older brother of tenor man Stanley was underrated during a fairly long career in jazz which saw him make successful contributions to records like this one and Sonny Clark's excellent *Leapin' and Lopin'* LP on Blue Note. His clear tone, open and muted, and ability to inject warmth, passion, pain or melancholy into the many different solos he played, made him a special, distinctive soloist although he tended to be overlooked at a time when extrovert performers like Lee Morgan, Freddie Hubbard and Donald Byrd were in the ascendancy. Warren and Higgins also made significant, hardy contributions and overall this disc brought 1961 to a close on a high note.

The next year was to see significant changes in Jackie's performance style and a move into what was called at the time 'the new thing', or 'free jazz'. McLean's contribution to the more freewheeling avant-garde jazz of the time has been misunderstood and it is surely worth making the point that his experimental music was always firmly grounded in the tradition and on what had gone before in the recent past.

He also went into a form of experimental, free jazz playing while retaining an insurance policy for himself and his record company by continuing to record in the old McLean style. As it turned out and, almost certainly with the musician's approval, these fail-safe recordings were kept on the shelf by Alfred Lion at Blue Note and did not see the light of day for at least fifteen years. It seems, with hindsight, that this was an intelligent, I might even say necessary, precaution for a musician prepared to go out on a limb seeking new avenues of expression and a radically different approach when he had established himself so firmly as a first rate, progressive hard bop soloist. Many jazz musicians, the majority in fact, develop and try to perfect a style and manner of playing and stick with it for the rest of their careers.

So, for the last two months of 1961 and most of 1962, Jackie McLean became the Dr. Jekyll (or Doctor Jackle) and Mr. Hyde of jazz if I can use such a description. To put it simply, the traditional, well-established Jekyll in McLean formed a quintet with trumpeter Kenny Dorham at the end of 1961 that played in the mainstream hard bop style. The band had successful engagements at the Jazz Workshop in San Francisco in November 1961 and the group recorded there live for United Artists Records (UAJ 15007). The quintet recorded again, with a different bassist and drummer, for Pacific Jazz (PJ 41) on April 15th 1962. A month earlier however, on March 19th 1962, Jackie McLean, or Mr. Hyde, had been into Van Gelder's studio in Englewood Cliffs with a very dissimilar quartet, comprising pianist Walter Davis Jr., bassist Herbie Lewis and drummer Billy Higgins to record *Let Freedom Ring* – very different music.

The earlier band represented the earlier Jackie – pianist Bobby Timmons, drummer Art Taylor and Dorham were some of the best of the hard bop musicians on the scene at the time and people that Jackie was as familiar with as they were with him. The United Artists and Pacific LPs were both very good and showed just how compatible Jackie was with Dorham but this was business as before (Jekyll) and the new Blue Note was after (Hyde). Make no mistake, many jazz folk were prepared and able to see plenty of evil in Mr. Hyde who dared to jeopardise a highly successful career as a hard bopper to move into unknown, avantgarde territory. I may be overstating it slightly but it is worth making the point that if highly gifted, forward-looking musicians like Rollins, Coltrane, Coleman, Dolphy and McLean had not been prepared to change direction and seek new methods and new avenues of expression, jazz would not have developed as rapidly and successfully as it did during the period between 1955 and the end of the 1960s. Not that Jackie strayed too far away from his roots, although it may have seemed at the time that he did.

McLean wrote his own liner notes for *Let Freedom Ring* and made it clear that while he credited Monk, Bird, Diz and Max Roach with a new concept of jazz and the start of freedom in improvisation, he was now looking towards Ornette Coleman. He also cited Coltrane, Mingus, Cecil Taylor, Dorham, Miles Davis, Sonny Rollins and Ellington as musicians who had taken that 'one step beyond'. Although this was to become the title of his next issued Blue Note LP, his own first step beyond was undoubtedly *Let Freedom Ring*.

It must have taken a lot of rehearsal, both time paid for by Blue Note and some in their own time, to prepare for this music. He was busy in this period playing live engagements even if it meant frequently going out of town to play one nighters, and he picked up on as many of these concerts and performances as he could. A musician as good and as resourceful as McLean was at this time was always going to find live gigs. But this new music was different, it was a departure and it was fortunate that Jackie was contracted to Blue Note rather than the more austere Prestige where he would never have had time to put such a session together or, just as importantly, prepare for it before going into the studio.

Jackie's liner notes state his opinion that 'emotion had taken an important step in expression' through the saxophone. Not that his work prior to 1962 had lacked emotive content but perhaps he felt that his new playing carried an excess charge of emotional blowing. He went on to express his frustration at not being able to play earlier compositions like 'A Fickle Sonance' and 'Quadrangle' in the correct manner while fully expressing himself. He had used 'I Got Rhythm' changes for 'Quadrangle' which, he felt, did not fit well and he had gone on, more recently, to employ sections of scales and modes. 'I try to write each thing with its own personality,' he stated. 'I choose the outstanding notes of the composition and build a scale or a motif to fit the feeling of the tune.' Later in the same liner note he talked about the deep respect he had for Miles Davis, his early employer and first real booster, who certainly manifested a deep influence starting early in the late 1940s and culminating in 1959 with his groundbreaking masterpiece *Kind of Blue*. This would most likely have been the record that Jackie studied in depth and realised that the scales and modes used by Miles could work equally well for him. From that point on he would use scales more and more and he seems to have decided on a fairly radical change of approach with regard to sound.

Let Freedom Ring sounds like no other record by Jackie McLean up to that point. Listening to it carefully we become aware that his tone, hard but emotive, has taken on an extra dimension, the high-pitched squeals that he inserts into his solos being the most obvious. The use of scales gives a three part modal structure to 'Omega' and 'Rene', the latter named for his eldest son.

It is basically a twelve bar blues but is here given a very contemporary interpretation. 'Melody for Melonae', which kicks off the record, is a variation of his earlier 'Little Melonae' written for his daughter, six years old at the time this session was recorded. It has, according to Jackie's own description, 'three different moods, first the melody, then it moves to a bright B-flat minor mode as a basis for solos. Each solo ends with a ballad section.'

This opening selection presented a brand new band sound and an even more ferocious and hard-swinging Jackie McLean to his public. From the dark opening piano chords from Walter Davis and the intense, acerbic opening saxophone notes, we know this is a new, contemporary Jackie, a musician seeking new methods of expression. The leader's solo is headlong, ever searching for fresh inventive devices and he is just about matched in invention and intensity by Billy Higgins' driving drum commentary. Higgins turns up the heat, supplying a myriad selection of rhythmic counter lines and tracing the alto solo throughout its length with just the right amount of interplay. This two-way conversation reminded me of the way John Coltrane and Elvin Jones would conduct a similar duo performance, each responding to the other as piano and bass faded away in the background. Davis and Lewis do not fade away completely here but the emphasis is fairly and squarely on alto sax and drums.

Davis follows the leader with a complex but flowing piano solo as Higgins provides a very slightly modified but still hard swinging rhythmic backup. The ballad sections are dark, misterioso, and yet curiously fresh and compelling.

Bud Powell's rich ballad 'I'll Keep Loving You' provides the leader with a tart but compellingly lyrical alto exploration. He is backed by Walter Davis' muscular piano chords and although this is the most conventional track on the disc, it still comes across as very much 'new' McLean rather than the familiar hard bop role he was famous for. High-pitched, orgiastic squeals are once again employed at key moments and he uses the full range of his instrument, occasionally swooping down into the basement, as Lester Young used to phrase it. Higgins' urgent cymbal splashes add to the force and gravity of this reading. Jackie's closing coda here is emotive: a heartfelt cry for love lost and not recovered.

'Rene' is, as noted, a much more conventional blues performance with McLean and Higgins once again prominent in a surging reading. As sleevenote annotator for the Rudy Van Gelder edition of this CD Bob Blumenthal notes: 'The still controversial McLean sound was never more acidic than on *Let Freedom Ring*.' It was Blumenthal too, who pointed out that the high upper register screams were executed 'with a precision of shading and pitch that should dispel any notions of random squealing.' I've never been fully convinced about this myself but over the years have become accustomed to those sounds and feel now that they fit the music. Then again it may just be that my ears have become used to those sounds through constant repetition, listening to the record. In any event the even harder, gritty tone, the adventurous improvising, the use of modes and frequent changes of tempo, signalled a brand new, probing and exploratory Jackie McLean, a musician who was, like his early idol Charlie Parker, pushing at the boundaries and seeking new directions for modern jazz to travel.

How would his many fans and supporters react: would they be turned off by the new McLean, claiming that he was playing an unintelligible music? Or would they happily embrace the new sounds and praise his adventurous spirit and invention? As it happened, he and Alfred Lion had made provision against the possibility that his fans would be turned off by the new music and would desert him and it.

12

ONE STEP FORWARD, ONE STEP BACK

A year after recording *Let Freedom Ring* (BLP 4106), McLean recorded and released *One Step Beyond* where the music moved even further out into free territory. But just three months after 4106, on June 14th 1962, he went into Van Gelder's studio to make what was listed in some Blue Note catalogues as *The Jackie McLean Quintet* (Blue Note 4116). It was not released at the time and only came to light in 1978 when it appeared under the original title in Japan and was issued in the U.S.A. as *Hipnosis* in the Blue Note Classic series, (BN-LA 483-J) together with another unissued McLean session from February 1967.

There seems little room for doubt now, at a distance of some fifty years, that this session was designed as a safety valve for McLean and Blue Note in case *Let Freedom Ring* did not sell and his reputation began to dissolve. Particularly so as a second, shall we say more traditional, session was recorded in 1962 and that too was left in the vaults for nearly twenty years. The fact that neither of these bop-orientated discs was issued at the time and they only came out years later speaks volumes for the success of McLean's new music and the sales those discs must have achieved in the early to mid-1960s. The two boppish sessions were excellent: Jackie McLean at his considerable bop and blues best.

The June 14th 1962 set picked up where *A Fickle Sonance* had left off, employing that special rhythm section of Sonny Clark, bassist Butch Warren and drummer Billy Higgins. Clark had a way of playing old-style swinging bop that seemed almost archaic when compared to the likes of Andrew Hill and Cecil

Taylor, both very active in contemporary jazz at that time, but with a hip swagger, a smoothness and flow to his delivery and such an easy, unforced swing that he somehow sounded as contemporary as anyone wanted to get. It was, literally, hard bop for the sixties filtered through the Bud Powell, Thelonious Monk bop of the forties and with an extra, indefinable ingredient of his own. Warren and Higgins were accomplished swingers and soloists and the drummer had worked with Ornette Coleman's original quartet, making him a much in demand modern accompanist. It should be no surprise to anybody that Jackie's front-line partner was trumpeter Kenny Dorham, a musician with whom he had teamed up in 1961, formed a quintet, and played live dates around the country. The musicians for these dates, apart from the two leaders, were Walter Bishop Jr. (piano), Art Taylor (drums) and Leroy Vinnegar on bass.

Listening today to what would have been Blue Note 4116, it is obvious that this is one of McLean's very best bop sessions, better I think, overall, than *Fickle Sonance* and not very far behind *Bluesnik* and *Jackie's Bag*. Had he not been heading in a fresher, more free direction it is almost inconceivable that an LP as good as this would not have been released soon after completion. It has often been said that McLean helped to establish the young, free jazz scene of the day by lending the weight of his reputation to the new music. He was one of the very first to record free style music for Blue Note in 1961 although, once his two LPs had been issued, several others followed, notably by people like trombonist Grachan Moncur III, a McLean discovery, and young Tony Williams who was first employed in NYC and recorded with Jackie and pianist Andrew Hill. So the new sound was officially on Blue Note and discs like 4116 were left in the vaults.

It was to be just about the last full-blooded, intense, no holds barred, hard bop disc that Jackie would make and what a swan song it turned out to be! By 1962 hard bop had gone through such a process of development, refinement and rigorous attention to the basics of jazz that the best examples fairly sizzled and burned. Soloists like Jackie had learned their craft listening to or playing with the likes of Parker, Bud Powell, Thelonious Monk and Lester Young, and studying, practising and refining their sounds and styles until they could play them pretty much in their sleep. It sometimes even appeared that they were doing precisely that when they almost nodded off but then came round in a hurry and blasted out solos so fierce and brimming with invention and passion that they seemed to heat up the walls of the club or studio. And as Ben Sidran pointed out in the sleevenote to *Hipnosis*, this hipness was part of the drug culture and pace of life in New York City. Talking about the drug connection Sidran said: 'Like all opiates heroin relaxes the individual. The combination of this enforced cool and the intense desire of young artists to prove themselves, created a tension in the music that was almost a signature of life in New York; energy burst through the music, but in a different, off-handed manner.' Sidran described the sound of hard bop at this time as 'furious, passionate indifference'.

Certainly the heroin must have helped the more skilled and emotive players like McLean and Clark to play to their limits and ride a slashing, almost killing rhythmic tempo without fear of stumbling or missing a beat. The relaxation of the drug would have bolstered their confidence and the rest would have been taken care of by their technical dexterity and artistic invention. And with a rhythm section like the Clark, Warren, Higgins unit, nobody coasted and nobody slacked off, not that soloists of the calibre of McLean and Dorham would have even contemplated giving less than one hundred percent effort.

The music on BLP 4116 kicks off with 'The Three Minors' a hard-burning piece of bop although it is built on three scales, each played for four bars giving a continuously turning circle, so it is an indication of the way Jackie was thinking by this time and a pointer to the music he would be playing throughout the rest of the 1960s. Everybody is on top form, Jackie's alto sound searing, full of pain, joy and frustration all mixed up into one glorious, almost heartbreaking sound. Clark is elegance personified but the crystalline beauty of his lines never obscures the fact that he is constantly driving forward, swinging the unit, as indeed are Warren and Higgins in tandem with him. Dorham plays with conviction and that unique, lyrical sound of his; he and Miles Davis had a similar style and conception of trumpet playing in those days, but Dorham lacked Davis' charisma and innovative force as a leader and shaper of music and musicians and managed to get himself consigned to history as an also-ran. He was much more than that as records like this demonstrate so effectively.

'Blues in A Jiff' is by Clark and probably, as the title suggests, put together in the studio at a moment's notice but these musicians could do that easily and this recording results in superior performance and stinging solos on an old, basic format. 'Blues for Jackie' is, as Ben Sidran's notes point out, much like a Horace Silver head, complete with brisk ensemble work tightly interwoven into rhythm breaks. Then there is a Billy Higgins composition, 'Marilyn's Dilemma', with the drummer providing a fascinating rhythmic platform for the soloists to shine on; 'Iddy Bitty' is followed by another McLean-penned blues, and the closing 'The Way I Feel' which cruises along in brisk, biting hard bop mode to round out the set. It formed Jackie's valediction to the hard bop style he had played and loved for years and he would not return to it for many, many years to come.

That however was on records. Between recording *Let Freedom Ring* in March 1962 and the quintet date (4116) in June, he was playing club dates with the group he co-led with Dorham and he recorded, under Kenny's leadership, *Matador* (United Artists UAJ 15007) on April 15th 1962 with a group comprising Bobby Timmons, bassist Teddy Smith and drummer J. C. Moses. The music here, although in the bop tradition, is based on South American music, inspired by a trip to that country by Dorham in 1961. The modal flavour of 'El Matador' which opens proceedings would have suited McLean well at this time but overall this is not one of either McLean's or Dorham's best or most representative discs. Much better all round was the disc they recorded together at the Jazz Workshop in San Francisco in November 1961, which features strong playing by the principals: Walter Bishop, Art Taylor and Leroy Vinnegar. The session consists mostly of standards, played with burning, hard bop vigour and, possibly, representing one of Jackie's last fully committed live sets in that style of playing.

There was however, yet another recording session for Blue Note which did not appear at the time but surfaced late in 1984. *Tippin' the Scales*, (Blue Note BST 84427) was recorded on September 28th 1962 and back on board were old pals Sonny Clark and Butch Warren, with Art Taylor taking over from Higgins on drums. This was a most relaxed session, unlike the almost ferocious 4116 with the quartet tackling laid-back, medium tempo pieces such as Jackie's 'Rainy Blues' and Clark's 'Nursery Blues', the latter a cute blues treatment of nursery rhymes. Then there were sturdy but basically still relaxed performances of 'Two For One' (which certainly contained hints of the music that was soon to come), the gentle 'Nicely' and a smooth ballad reading of 'Cabin in the Sky'.

Although it does not conform to any specific style and is, perhaps, not typical of his playing at the time, *Tippin' the Scales* is a very fine record and one of Jackie's rare, and much to be treasured, quartet dates. He is the main soloist and he makes the most of it with only Clark's resilient, melodic but essentially brief solos as contrast. The result is an offbeat but thoroughly enjoyable McLean record and again it seems highly likely that it would have been released if the altoist had not been in the process of setting off in new directions.

So, apart from the two discs with the shortly to break up but regularly working Dorham quintet, Jackie's only issued LP for Blue Note in 1962 was *Let Freedom Ring*. And as the other two, more conventional discs languished in the vaults he began preparing for his next issued LP *One Step Beyond* by working club dates and concerts with some of the bright young free players of the day, musicians like Grachan Moncur, the trombonist who would become a member of Jackie's more permanent band in 1963–65.

Jackie was able to take time to plan, rehearse and finally record his two new music albums with confidence as he was under contract to Blue Note. As in the past, he tended to play and record wherever possible with a fair number of young, upcoming musicians although he would always tend to strengthen any band he worked in with gifted, experienced professionals like Doug Watkins and Paul Chambers on bass, and Art Taylor, Philly Joe Jones and Billy Higgins on drums. He was also about to meet and introduce to the world of professional jazz music a young drummer of extraordinary ability, Tony Williams, who would work and record with him before departing to become a member of one of the most celebrated rhythm sections of all time.

* * *

In the May 1962 issue of *Jazz Monthly*, Michael James wrote his second feature on the musician he had praised and brought to many people's attention in December 1959.[1] In an appreciative and informative essay about McLean he reiterates his view that the altoist was no mere copyist of Charlie Parker, an opinion much prevalent at the time on both sides of the Atlantic. James concedes that critical opinion had, by 1962, begun to swing in favour of the importance and originality of McLean's work as a soloist and he analyses four of his Blue Note LPs and concludes that he had grown considerably as a soloist but, with a few exceptions, was less venturesome, harmonically and tonally on other leaders' albums than on his own dates. Two of the exceptions James mentions are Lee Morgan's *Leeway* on Blue Note BLP 4034 and Donald Byrd's *Fuego*. I am in compete agreement with James both in his assessment of McLean's general playing as a sideman and in the exceptions that these two releases represent. In particular Jackie's solos on 'Midtown Blues' and 'The Lion and the Wolf' from the Morgan disc stand out as searing, highly charged modern blues solos, their intensity rarely, if ever matched on alto sax since the days of Charlie Parker at his peak.

James had been corresponding with Jackie for some time and the two met when McLean travelled to London to appear in *The Connection*. His music may have been in a state of flux with attempts to move out into the free area juxtaposed with a fair amount of playing in the old hard bop manner but he was confident in his own abilities and appeared content with the way things were going. He told James that Miles Davis and Thelonious Monk were the two musicians who were then having the greatest effect on his own style. The Davis influence was undoubtedly in the economy of notes he employed on his later records, in contrast to the early Prestige and Ad Lib sessions in the mid-fifties. Monk's influence, as James observed, 'has been more keenly felt in the spheres of rhythm – the displacement of notes from their expected positions, the movement of a phrase across the beat, and so on.'

Michael James' essay is valuable because it gives us glimpses of Jackie McLean in 1962, a time when his music was very much in the ascendancy but he himself was little known and rarely, if ever, featured in interviews in the jazz press or newspapers. He spoke to James about his enthusiasm for Sonny Rollins and John Coltrane and confided that his son, Rene, had studied saxophone with the former. He also indicated that he thought many of his early records were spoilt by a lack of rehearsal but also told James how important he felt spontaneity and freedom of expression were. Balancing those two must have occupied a good deal of Jackie's early musical development but he certainly came through as a wild, yet disciplined, original voice whose music always sounded freshly minted and as personal as you can get.

James also found the altoist uncompromising in his likes and dislikes, reporting that Jackie had expressed his contempt for a musician who, at the time, was fashionable and very popular. James would not name the musician but later spoke about McLean refusing to cash in on the gospel craze and solve his economic problems in that manner when 'many less able performers' have done so. In contrast, Jackie expressed great admiration for Art Blakey, Paul Chambers, Art Taylor and trumpeter Blue Mitchell, all of them having featured on one or more of his recordings and most likely played in live venues with him.

James ended his essay with quotes from soprano saxophonist Steve Lacy, one of the very best and most technically well-equipped of the new, avant-garde players. Lacy picked out Coltrane, Rollins, Ben Webster, Ornette Coleman, Johnny Hodges and McLean in his list of the contemporary saxophonists whose work most interested him. According to Lacy at that time, Jackie had 'the most rhythmic vitality and, so far, the least discipline of all these saxophonists. He expresses his own personality with his sound and has tremendous swing and energy.' James pointed out that Lacy's comments had been made in 1959 and added that Jackie had made significant strides in suppressing unnecessary detail within his phrases and controlling their shapes over the course of a lengthy solo to make for a more durable effect.

This essay, along with the available recorded music, gives a good insight into the progress of McLean at the time and James did not believe he had yet given the final measure of his potential. He was right about that.

13

ONE STEP BEYOND

On 30th April 1963 McLean recorded *One Step Beyond* (BST 84137) for Blue Note and, apart from a significant move away from hard bop and into more adventurous free territory, the recording signified the beginning of a number of important changes in his life. Most importantly of all, from a personal viewpoint and for the benefit of his wife and children, he managed to become drug free and leave behind the horrors of addiction to heroin. 'I'm a family man and a musician,' he told Ken Burns in 1996, 'so my life wasn't that different from Bird's, but it has to do with who your wife is and who your family is and it's terrible, you know.' He had referred earlier to the trials and tribulations that Parker faced when he spoke about addiction being a part of your life, not separate. He mentioned getting up, sick, his body craving the drug and having to go out and buy it, 'to relieve your body ache, of the pain, of the sickness you have when you are addicted to a drug like heroin.' Ostensibly talking about Charlie Parker, he was, of course, talking just as much about himself, his own pain and sickness and the effect on his family.

Jackie had endured eighteen years of continuous addiction at this time and had just about had enough. By the time he went into the studio to record *One Step Beyond* he had made up his mind to quit using heroin. He talked at the time to reporters about considering his wife and mother and kids and complained that he had a gorilla on his back and had needed to wrestle with it every day.

It was a painfully honest assessment of his own and his family's plight and, unlike some high profile jazz musicians of Jackie's generation, he did not go to great lengths to deny it or try to keep it quiet or pretend that it never happened. Many did, and they worked hard to keep it from the public domain. For those who were always addicted until death claimed them, no matter how little they used, it seems a pointless exercise. Honesty was always McLean's policy in music and honesty in all his dealings with life and commerce would see him through a career as a jazz soloist and later as an educator, that became progressively more impressive and distinguished. Yes, he had led a wild life as a youth and yes, he had been under the influence of Charlie Parker's way of life and he had paid the price. Nobody emerges unscathed from a long period as an addict and, coming up in the times he did, taking the drug would have affected the way he played, the sound he got and the mixed emotions he poured into his music in the late 1950s and early 1960s.

Gradually, through a series of events in the early 1960s in which giving up heroin was of prime importance, he would enter a new phase where he would form and play with a regular band. This had not happened, he informed us in the liner notes to *One Step Beyond*, since 1958.

Jackie said that after *The Connection* closed in 1962 following a four-year-run he started to get calls for jobs for club or concert work around NYC.[1] He claimed that he had employed a wide range of first rate musicians but on a one-off basis and that getting the right musicians together to form a band was never easy, 'especially if you want to acquire a different sound'. What was not said but probably very relevant at the time was that keeping even a very good band working regularly was almost impossible at that time. He had found it almost impossible to maintain a group with such talents as Mal Waldron, George Tucker, on bass and Larry Ritchie on drums. Add in the additional problems of having to scuffle around to get heroin and all the attendant grief that situation imposes and it is easy to see why McLean settled for freelance playing with pickup rhythm sections so frequently between 1956 and the close of *The Connection*.

Having made his name as both a top jazz soloist and an actor in the play, it was ironic that he was still living the life of one of the characters in the play on the streets of New York in having to find his own connection and get access to the drug, although he worked regularly. The turning point appears to have come around the time he went to Boston with a week's booking at Connelly's club. He was to be the soloist with a local rhythm section, a situation that was as familiar to him as night following day. The key phrase above was, of course, 'especially if you want to acquire a different sound'. Jackie had realised that he could play hard bop, that most durable and consistent jazz style forever and a day and always find plenty of good musicians to back him as a rhythm section. Just about every jazz musician in NYC, apart from those few who still clung to the old New Orleans style, could play bop or hard bop. But Jackie was looking for a new challenge, ready to stretch and even break boundaries, searching for a new way of expressing himself through his music; this would need musicians with a similar outlook and he would only start to achieve his goals with a regular, working band.

The catalysts for the new sound appear to have been trombonist Grachan Moncur and drummer Tony Williams. McLean told the story in the liner notes to *One Step Beyond* of when he was rushing to get to an engagement in Boston early 'to rehearse the section and get some originals set up'. He arrived and was helped with his bags by a young man who told him that the rhythm players were already up on the bandstand waiting for him. Jackie had sat down to catch his breath but was soon up again and asking the young man who he was playing with. Ray Santisi was the pianist, a reliable and busy Boston musician at that time, as was the bassist, John Neves. 'What about the drums?' he enquired. The young man answered 'Me – Tony

Williams – and I'm very happy to meet you Jackie.' Not surprisingly, Jackie was astonished and more than a little wary. He learned that the young man was just seventeen years old but also found out, to his delight, that he played exceptionally well and the whole week in Boston was very enjoyable for them all.

Luck or fate or something of the sort must also have played a part because it turned out that Williams, young as he was, was just the sort of drummer that McLean was looking for, or soon would be. Not a conventional straight-ahead bop player but an adventurous seeker of new horizons who could play softly with brushes, cook up a storm with complex and unconventional cross rhythms and break up the time constantly to set the music and musicians in new directions at a moment's notice. And before Jackie's gig in Boston had ended he was asking Williams if he could come to New York. Jackie sought and received the consent and blessing of Tony's mother and took him back to his house in NYC on Christmas Eve, 1962. *The Connection* was still running at that time and Jackie was retained as musical director. The two worked in *The Connection* until it closed and then followed up with some concerts and club appearances. This would have given McLean an added perspective on the precocious talent of the young drummer and the valuable weeks spent playing together would have indicated to McLean that Williams was just what he needed for the new, planned band.

Moncur, the young trombone player, had been an on-off associate of Jackie's since 1957. They had played together frequently in pick-up groups and often rehearsed together. Fortunately these two had similar outlooks on jazz and the way it should be played and developed in 1963 when, after a gap, they met up again in NYC. As McLean had a few gigs lined up he invited Moncur to join him and play and then, as Jackie wrote in his liner notes to *One Step Beyond*, they practised together at the altoist's house and soon discovered that they had similar ideas about composing jazz scores. 'I could really see that Grachan was a talented composer as well as musician,' Jackie reported and went on to say that Tony Williams always joined them at the practice sessions, bringing ideas and part of his kit to play along.

McLean had two weeks at the Coronet club in NYC coming up and he began to rehearse the new music with Moncur, Williams and Bobby Hutcherson on vibes. They tried out a few bassists but, in Jackie's words, 'things didn't lay right'. Then he phoned Eddie Khan, a bassist working with drummer Max Roach at that time and he fitted into the style and concept that the leader had in mind. With far more thoroughness and attention to detail than many bandleaders of the time, Jackie rehearsed the new compositions endlessly, played them at his next few gigs and then at the Coronet club for two weeks. And so what is heard on *One Step Beyond* is very similar to what would have been heard at the club at that time.

The record is an even more blatant example of outside playing than *Let Freedom Ring*. It starts with 'Saturday and Sunday', a modal piece by Jackie with an intense, probing, passionate alto solo in which pretty much the full range of his instrument is used. Spurred on and propelled forward by the erratic, spiky interjections from Hutcherson and particularly Williams, this really sounds like jazz of the future even if it has landmarks and strong roots in the past and present. Moncur's trombone solo is almost as fiery and futuristic as the leader's and Hutcherson keeps the fires burning on his solo segment. Listening to this track today it sounds as contemporary as any jazz I've heard in the past few months so what effect it must have had on unwary listeners in 1963 is difficult to imagine. Williams plays fragmented, rolling cross rhythms in a jerky solo towards the end and it is no surprise that shortly after this the young drummer was recruited by Miles Davis for his second great quintet rhythm section.

Jackie described 'Frankenstein' by Moncur as one of the most beautiful jazz waltzes he had ever heard. 'Its beauty stands for everything Frankenstein does not.' Again the leader's alto solo is supercharged and highly emotional, spewing out more of the high register squeals that had been so prevalent on *Let Freedom Ring*. Moncur follows with a neat, tidily constructed solo and Hutcherson produces what is arguably the best of the three. Jackie points out in the notes that his two front-line colleagues are searching for what they hear and see. After acknowledging the obvious influence of Milt Jackson on his sideman, he continues: 'You can hear Bobby's own expression and conception emerging fat on all these sides.' The steady three quarter time is held and smoothly maintained throughout by Williams and Khan.

'Blue Rondo' is a B-flat blues written by McLean and the most straight-ahead track on the disc. The final track, 'Ghost Town' by Moncur, is the most atmospheric and original composition on the record. Slow and mournful, the wailing sax and trombone, dissonant cries from the horns at appropriate moments and all sorts of strange, spooky rattles and scrapes from the drum kit make the listener think that he or she is listening to activity in a ghost town. Jackie's solo contains all the emotive pathos and yearning he is capable of mustering – a considerable amount indeed.

Two important points emerge from this recording: one is that Jackie was more than ready to pursue new sounds and new directions for the immediate future. He had, on this recording, already proved that the best of the avant-garde jazz of the time had to be disciplined and had to pay regard to tradition in the way it was written and interpreted. In this respect he was the ideal veteran player who had mastered both the old and the new styles of jazz and would provide a role model for young musicians just starting out and unsure how to proceed. The second point is that in Williams and Moncur he had the basis of his first regular quintet since 1955–56 and a chance of keeping a group together for some time. He could not have known that Miles would spoil his plan to some extent by snatching away the precociously talented seventeen-year-old Tony Williams but that, perhaps, was inevitable. Few drummers had both considerable technical expertise and a truly original sound and approach and if it hadn't been Davis taking him, another top flight bandleader would have coaxed him away with equal offers of money that McLean, at that time, could not match.

The new Jackie McLean however was fully established with *One Step Beyond*. The inspiration of Ornette Coleman and Miles Davis' explorations of archaic modes may have given him a fresh, new lease of life and a desire to explore new avenues, as seen in *Let Freedom Ring*. But it was *One Step Beyond* that saw him consolidate his new approach and come up with four new, highly engaging compositions – two by himself and two by Moncur – and, indeed, a new band and a whole new sound. Where *Let Freedom Ring* had sounded like an intriguing and exciting experiment, *One Step Beyond* sounded like the finished, successful article. Ending his liner notes, the leader said, 'I am looking forward to my next date with this band. Playing with Grachan, Khan, Bobby and Tony is a real pleasure. I said earlier that staying away from a rut and finding newer and freer material is part of my inspiration to play and write.'

Just before the recording of *One Step Beyond*, McLean had gone into the Van Gelder studio in February 1963 to record a quintet date with Donald Byrd, Herbie Hancock, Butch Warren and Tony Williams (*Vertigo*, BN LT-1085). It was not released at the time. Feverish recording activity was going on at Blue Note and, in this case, one of his more 'outside' sessions was being consigned to the vaults and would not get a release until the late 1970s when Liberty Records, which then owned the company, released it on their programme of reissues in the LT series. Marketed as Jazz Classics they were, in fact, previously overlooked or even rejected material. It is difficult to pin down exactly why so much material did not see the light of day at the time of recording; Alfred Lion always maintained that they were so busy in the 1960s that many recordings were forgotten or temporarily lost. My own feeling is that although they wanted to keep the musicians busy and enjoyed working with them and recording them frequently, Lion and Wolff were running a small independent company on a very limited budget and simply could not afford to put out everything.

The 1963-64 period was crucial to the development and change in Jackie McLean's music. A chain of events began which saw him link up with two forward-thinking musicians and set him in the direction of forming a more permanent band and not relying on work as a single with pick-up rhythm sections. Having recorded with Moncur and the others he was ready to work with them regularly and this is what he did. Following on from this, with the responsibility for running a band with three or four other musicians dependent on him, he had a strong inducement to take the giant step of giving up the use of hard drugs and this he achieved sometime in 1964. From this point on he would be free of that gorilla and, in addition to being one of the most important alto stylists since Parker, he would start to concentrate on recruiting and helping more and more young musicians. At first he just gave them sidemen jobs in his combos, as he had done since the mid-fifties but, gradually, a new McLean was emerging: an educator, a music teacher who would start and run a jazz education programme that is still running successfully today, and is a fitting epitaph to the saxophonist.

14

DESTINATION – OUT

Although he spent a good twenty years or more playing bop and hard bop and it could be described as his overall favourite jazz format, McLean was thinking in terms of expanding his craft and looking for new means of expression as early as the mid-1950s. Parker had advised him to listen to Stravinsky and after Bird died Jackie took this advice. He said that it opened his head to a lot of other concepts of playing, like that of Sun Ra and Cecil Taylor. He later talked about music that had an open concept and described it as a place where you could cross a threshold and have no barriers, no key signatures, no chord progressions, no particular form. Then he heard Ornette Coleman late in 1959 and began to question the old methods when here was a sax player free to blow in any manner he fancied, and giving his sidemen freedom to follow him or branch out on their own. He did admit to being 'a little leery' of the people who followed Ornette but was convinced by the way Coleman had stood his ground, withstood all the harsh, bitter criticism and had shown that his music could work.

So the seeds of the new free music that Jackie would embrace so enthusiastically in the early 1960s, were already being sown in the 1950s and after hearing Miles' *Kind of Blue* he must have been entertaining his first thoughts of how using scales might help in the playing of some of his own more complex compositions.

Even though it now seems most likely that the quintet and quartet records of 1962 which were not released at the time were intended as safeguards against the possible failure of the new music, this alone does not explain the feverish recording activity that went on at Blue Note throughout the 1960s and into the 1970s, bearing in mind that the policy of frequent recording but only issuing a small percentage of everything put on tape was continued by the Liberty/United Artists group when they owned the company from 1965. It is true that Blue Note as a company from the time of McLean's *Let Freedom Ring* release were operating a policy of releasing both straight-ahead and free music although most of the straight-ahead releases delayed the free dates and vice versa.

Take the case of trumpeter Lee Morgan, a regular associate and frequent fellow front-liner with Jackie. His adventurous and fairly progressive disc, *Search for the New Land*, had to wait a year for release because the unexpected and almost overwhelming success of *The Sidewinder* caused Blue Note to rush out a follow-up, *The Rumproller*, in the same bop and blues style. McLean fared better with his more progressive music going out first and the more hard boppish sessions waiting in the vaults.

One Step Beyond, released in 1963, was the first time that Tony Williams had been heard on records, but it was not the first session that he recorded. As noted earlier, on February 11th he had recorded five tracks on the quintet date that became known as the *Vertigo* session when it was eventually released. Jackie had recorded this date with old friends Donald Byrd and Butch Warren and with Williams on drums. The future Miles Davis rhythm section pianist Herbie Hancock was at the keyboard. Allowing for the feverish activity going on at Blue Note at the time and Lion's attempts to serve the music and the musicians well, this one's non appearance might make sense. Like many others it was probably all ready to go in April when McLean recorded *One Step Beyond*. That record contained well-written, exceptionally well-played new music; an obvious move outside and a change in direction for the altoist that was to have far reaching consequences. The *Vertigo* session was not out-and-out free jazz; rather it was a curious mixture of free and bop. The title track is almost like a practice rundown for the tracks on *One Step Beyond* with the altoist fashioning a long, extended improvisation with no settled chord structure and driving support from Hancock, Warren and Williams. It is a strong statement in terms of contemporary jazz of the day, far more advanced than most and in line with what Coleman, Eric Dolphy and a very few others were achieving at the time. The next track, however, 'Cheers', is a straight-ahead bop vehicle with far more conventional playing; McLean takes the A melody and Donald Byrd takes the B and the rhythm section cooks merrily in time honoured fashion. 'Yams', which ends side two on the original LP release, is a slow, funky blues which glides along attractively with that after-hours feel and is similar to the sort of blues lines that Horace Silver was writing and recording with the original Jazz Messengers, way back in 1954–55.

Overall it is a very good session but it does mix styles and the presence of Byrd probably encouraged the leader to keep the music rather more conservative than most that he was playing. Byrd was, at the time, very much a hard bop man but the two had been friends since their days with George Wallington's quintet back in 1955 and Jackie's first record as a leader in the same year. The record was maybe seen to fall between two musical stools and left on the shelf for that reason. In the long term, however, it can been seen as a vital link in the development of McLean's music between 1961 and the rest of that decade.

Jackie's main sphere of activity was still the quintet with Moncur, Hutcherson and Williams, a group that was mutually inspiring. Hutcherson had first become involved when he met Jackie at a rehearsal at bassist Herbie Lewis' apartment. Hutcherson and McLean soon became friends and the vibist took Blue Note boss Alfred Lion to hear the new group at the Coronet when they had their first gig there. Lion was very enthusiastic and according to Hutcherson he was keen to record

Jackie with his new sound,[1] so there we have another clue indicating that it might well have been Lion who initiated the release of more 'outside' music from Jackie in the initial stages.

In any event the first LP sold fairly well and five months after the recording of *One Step Beyond* he returned to Van Gelder's Englewood Cliffs studio to record *Destination – Out* (BLP 84165), a session along the same lines as the April disc and with almost the same personnel. Tony Williams must have already been courted by Miles Davis by this time and his place was taken by Roy Haynes, a veteran drummer of impeccable pedigree who could play in every jazz style from dixieland to free. Haynes, a master drummer in terms of technique and the ability to swing any combo, had played with Louis Armstrong, Lester Young and Sarah Vaughan, and was the alternative drummer of choice in Coltrane's quartet when Elvin Jones was taking a rest at the government's pleasure. In his liner notes to the initial LP release, Jackie described Haynes as 'a living example of a jazz musician's progress with the times'. He also described him as an all-round drummer who had been on the scene for many years, worked with Bud Powell in the 1940s and played frequently with Charlie Parker. He had obviously picked the ideal replacement in a musician so versatile and adaptable but he must have felt aggrieved that Williams, one of the bright young lights of jazz drumming in the early sixties, had left him so quickly and so suddenly. Jackie had brought him to New York, entertained him over Christmas at home with his family and then employed him while he was still a teenager and given him his first record dates on Blue Note. From Williams' point of view, it is perhaps understandable that the chance to progress, as he would have seen it, and become part of one of the great rhythm sections in jazz must have been overwhelming. Not that he would have known at the time that the section would become so prominent and influential but in fairness to him, his talent was to play a big part in the fashioning and development of that great rhythm trio.

Destination – Out featured the same group as *One Step Beyond* except for the change of drummer and Larry Ridley replacing Eddie Khan on bass. The instrumental balance was the same with the trombone and alto front line providing a dark, rich sound seldom heard in jazz previously. Hutcherson fulfilled the 'chordal instrument' role admirably and his freewheeling lines and open-minded choice of chords most likely suited the front-line players much better than a fairly conventional pianist would have done. In any case it was the sound that Jackie wanted and had heard in his head prior to them playing a note together. Jackie noted in his sleevenote that the recording session had started out almost 'in the same vein as *One Step Beyond*'; rehearsals were set up between him, Hutcherson and Moncur and the three musicians: 'ironed out the rough spots in about a week and a half'. It gives a good insight into the way McLean was thinking and working at that time: first get the ideal front line, in this case alto, trombone and vibes, an unusual combination to start with, then write and rehearse new material and, finally, choose a bassist and drummer who are advanced and open to new ideas and will follow you wherever you venture. The last may not have been a conscious thing at the time but Jackie would have known that it would work well that way especially as Hutcherson would function as a first-rate soloist and rhythm section player.

The leader praised Moncur's composition 'Love and Hate' in his liner, describing it as 'using very few notes and yet one detects loneliness, sadness and beauty, each blending and standing apart from the other; a true work of art.' It is Jackie's own heart-wrenching alto solo that sets the mood and emphasizes the loneliness, sadness and beauty he speaks about so convincingly. This dark, rather sombre ballad is very effective as the opening track with stand-out solos from McLean, Moncur, Hutcherson and Ridley. An aura of almost passionate despair seems to hang over the piece and the blend of alto, trombone and vibes is eerily, lyrically effective.

The next track 'Esoteric', again written by the trombonist, is another strangely original-sounding piece, moving crisply from 3/4 to 4/4 time and again emphasising the unusual but striking blend of the three front-line instruments. Jackie's stop-start solo is fragmentary but effective, especially when he gets into his 4/4 swinging passages. The leader wrote 'Kahlil the Prophet' which is more of a straight-ahead swinger with everybody in top form and particularly Hutcherson who combines an original choice of notes with a hard but free-flowing swing, aided and encouraged by Ridley and Haynes. There are rhythm variations in this piece as Jackie points out in his liner note but it stays in 4/4 during the solo sections.

The session ends with 'Riff Raff', which McLean describes as 'a blues in disguise'. It is also a very relaxed, medium tempo swinger and brings the set to a more conventional conclusion. Everybody sounds laid-back here, as though the efforts of going far out in the more free compositions is being rewarded at the end by a basic, simple stroll through the blues, disguised or not.

It was records like *One Step Beyond* and *Destination – Out* that changed the perceptions of people like Alfred Lion and his partner Francis Wolff. Both were fairly heavily committed to bop and hard bop and the company was late getting to the free jazz style releases. By 1962, when Jackie released *Let Freedom Ring*, other companies had already put out 'New Wave' recordings, as they were called at the time: music by Ornette Coleman on Atlantic, Eric Dolphy on Prestige, Cecil Taylor on Candid and Contemporary and even lesser known composer/instrumentalists such as trumpeter Booker Little, whose *Out Front* showed a personal approach to the new music on his Candid LP. And, of course, once Jackie's Blue Note LPs were out there, in the record shops and selling reasonably well, it left the door open for others to be given a chance.

During those years from 1963 onwards, Blue Note recorded free style music by Cecil Taylor, Ornette Coleman, Eric Dolphy,

Grachan Moncur, Tony Williams and several other, lesser-known musicians, even though they insured themselves against possible failure with albums by Lou Donaldson, Jimmy Smith, Horace Parlan, Stanley and Tommy Turrentine, The Three Sounds and many other first-rate players who were still committed to hard bop and blues. There was room for both but if McLean hadn't started the ball rolling it might have taken years for Blue Note to get on the bandwagon.

The early 1960s were a time of transition and change for Jackie McLean that would herald a new maturity and much greater depth to his playing and composing. Although he never forgot hard bop or, indeed, stopped playing it for any length of time, the new music occupied his thoughts, his playing at gigs and recording sessions and kept his music fresh and vital throughout that decade. It all really started with *Let Freedom Ring*, one of the very best of his 1960s LPs, but it would gain fresh momentum and the start of a new lease of musical life with *One Step Beyond*. With these recordings he had taken his own personal 'one step beyond'.

15

ACTION

Jackie McLean's life changed considerably in the years from 1962 to the end of that decade and the changes were consistently positive. He began a programme of writing and playing that explored new territory and new sounds and ideas but never lost sight of his roots and the music he had come up with. Indeed he continued to play in the hard bop style, alternating more free performances with traditional hard bop sessions both live and on record.

1964 became a particular time of transition when, along with a consistent programme of recordings, both old and new style, he shook off the debilitating shackles of heroin addiction and took his first steps as an educator in Harlem. The case for getting off heroin was indisputable, no matter what, if any, benefits there were to his playing from the relaxation of being 'high'. Having a clear head and not needing to scuffle to get drug money freed him to concentrate all his creative energies, which were always considerable, on the two most important aspects of his life: his family and his music. As he acknowledged later, he could not have done it without the help and support of his wife, Dollie. The fact that he had spent fourteen years as an addict, many of them as a married man, speaks volumes for the strength of their relationship and, specifically, the backing and support she was prepared and able to give to him through those years.

His ambivalent attitude towards new trends in music shows that he was never completely seduced by the 'avant-garde' or 'free' styles but saw them as a necessary development, an extension to what he was doing that he could incorporate into his own playing. In any case he always saw the music of Ornette Coleman as a means of injecting freshness and vitality into jazz at a time when it had become fairly stagnant but he never regarded it as all that radical. Jackie often talked about music generally and Coleman's in particular at that time. Coleman's music was, he said, 'just good music or bad'. The title of 'the new thing' had been hung on Coltrane and Ornette but he doubted that Coleman was any newer than Charlie Parker. And he didn't think Coleman himself would think that he was. It was also said at the time that Jackie's 'conversion', if it could indeed be called that, gave the avant-garde an enormous boost when most of his contemporaries were screaming 'fraud'.[1]

McLean was looked up to by young musicians at the time as one who had paid all his dues and made it as a conventional soloist, and that in turn gave him great credibility with other musicians, young and old. Along with many lesser names that benefited directly, McLean gave employment opportunities to the likes of trumpeters Charles Tolliver and Woody Shaw, pianist Larry Willis, drummers Jack DeJohnette and Tony Williams and trombonist Grachan Moncur. There is an example of his impact in the words of alto saxophonist Gary Bartz: 'I always trusted McLean. If he said "I'm really looking into this new stuff," I wanted to look into it too.'[2] And that was the reaction of numerous other young musicians at the time and for many years afterwards.

McLean began to take the initial steps as an educator after his roles in the stage production and then in Shirley Clarke's film version of Jack Gelber's *The Connection*. After he left the Living Theatre in 1961, he gradually became involved with young people in trouble, first as a bandmaster in a penitentiary and later he began to contribute to programmes such as HARYOU-ACT (Harlem Youth Opportunities Unlimited–Associated Community Teams). Working in *The Connection* and noting the close parallels between his own life and his role in the play must surely have set him in the direction that led eventually to his kicking the habit permanently, although it did take him another two and a half years to complete.

The music at this time was, as usual, ambivalent. On August 11th 1964, Jackie was at Van Gelder's studio to play on a Lee Morgan session called *Tom Cat* (Blue Note LT 1058). He joined trombonist Curtis Fuller and a lively rhythm section that included McCoy Tyner and Art Blakey for a programme of straight-ahead bop and blues. There is no reason to suppose that he did not thoroughly enjoy recording these tracks; he was in the company of old pals and an ex-employer in Blakey, and his impassioned playing on the opening 'Tom Cat' is indication enough that this was no mere duty call. 'Exotique', which has time changes and moves into 6/8, is adventurous as a piece of writing by Morgan at the time although nowhere near as 'free' and explorative as McLean's music. Jackie is obviously still in his element here and on all of the tracks on this set; although he was exploring many new avenues on his own leader dates, he was more than happy to play in the older style he knew and loved so much. There is also evidence that although his music moved in many different directions throughout the 1960s and was relatively successful, he still retained that affection for his first love, bebop, which no other format ever eclipsed completely. But he did not like labels and objected to their use more than once. He was reported to have said 'I don't want to hear any more about bebop or hard bop or this or that category. Titles hang things up. The music is just good or bad.'[3]

The other point to be made is that this record, with Morgan, McLean and Tyner all on top form, not to mention the omnipresent Blakey, is one of the best Blue Note sessions of 1964 and once again, it is a mystery that it was not released at the time. The only possible explanation in this case is that, as the music on this session was similar to *Search for the New Land*, both that and *Tom Cat* were shelved and priority was given by the record company to such toe-tapping pot boilers as *The Sidewinder* and *The Rumproller*. *New Land* was released later in the year but *Tom Cat* was either forgotten or felt to be too close to that disc and it remained in the vaults for sixteen years. As one of the exuberant Morgan's best recordings, it should not have been withheld and it is highly recommended to anybody who has not heard it yet.

It was in 1964 that Jackie made his first trip to Japan, taking with him a band comprising Cedar Walton on piano, Reggie Workman, bass, Roy Haynes on drums and tenor saxophonist Benny Golson. This proved to be a very enjoyable and eye opening tour for McLean and his sidemen and he later told A. B. Spellman how much he had appreciated the attention and praise that had been heaped on them by the Japanese fans. Not for the first or last time would he enthuse about how good it felt to be appreciated for what he did, to have people listening attentively to his music in clubs and concert halls and coming round afterwards to ask to have album covers or tee shirts autographed. He told Spellman that he was impressed by being in a country that was not dominated by the Caucasian race. 'It's a different feeling,' he said, 'to go into another man's country and see a man with a closer colour relationship to you, running his own country and to watch the white man take the back seat, on the defence.'

There wasn't much of a club scene in Japan according to Jackie but the group played in concert halls in all the major cities and hundreds of people turned out to meet them at the various airports. 'They really are devoted jazz fans,' he said, recalling with surprise and delight the various enthusiastic receptions and, although unspoken, no doubt registering his feeling that this sort of appreciation of his music would go down very well in his homeland. It is certainly a theme he returned to many times over the years.

Coming down to earth with a bang he went home to the

United States and lost an appeal against a three-year-old narcotics conviction. He served six months in prison and was, according to Spellman, so traumatised by what went on there that he made up his mind that he would never go back and determined to beat his addiction to heroin. This was the start of a new phase of his life that would unfurl over the next few years.

On September 16th, McLean returned to Van Gelder's studio to record his own session, *Action* (Blue Note 4218). Unlike his previous four or five albums, this session seems to have caught him in two distinct moods, part of the material is in the 'free' style but some tracks are in the old hard bop format. Perhaps the answer can be found in the opening quote from him in the first paragraph of Nat Hentoff's sleevenotes on the initial LP release: 'I never want to go "outside" for too long a time without coming back "inside" again.' In other words he was hedging his bets, seeing how the new and old music fared but, as he played with such dedication, consistency and sheer passion to communicate his music to the listeners, he was always successful no matter what style he adopted. I sometimes think that if McLean had formed a New Orleans sextet at this time, with clarinet, trombone and possibly even a banjo and played alto in that style, he would have been successful.

The opening track on *Action* is very much in the then current McLean experimental style. As he himself described it, 'once the solo improvisations start there are no chord changes and no scales to follow. The soloist has to listen, therefore, to Bobby Hutcherson for leads to where to go.' McLean pointed out that Hutcherson did lay out a lot but every once in a while he 'comes in and points a new direction, and then he cuts the soloist loose again.'

After the solid commitment to free style on records like *Let Freedom Ring* and *One Step Beyond*, it is soon obvious that *Action* represents both traditional and new styles. The disc contains a typically original reading of 'I Hear a Rhapsody' by McLean, a song he claims in the liner notes that he was never able to master for years after hearing Charlie Parker play it so comprehensively. 'He had played it so completely, as if there were no more rhapsodies to listen for after that experience,' Jackie told Nat Hentoff. 'He really tore it up. But one night, a couple of years ago at the Coronet in Brooklyn, someone requested it, and I went to the mike and stated the melody. I played that melody over and over again until finally it came to me and I got inside the song.' He really gets inside the melody on this recording and it is a traditional version but boasting a fresh, vivid arrangement from the altoist.

Once again, as he had done with sidemen on previous discs, McLean shares composing duties with his front-line partner. 'Plight' and 'Wrong Handle' are intriguing originals by Charles Tolliver, a trumpet player championed by McLean at the time and featured live with him at clubs in NYC and Boston. Jackie contributed 'Action' and 'Hootnan' which he describes as 'a blues without being a blues'. He explained that it featured twelve bar phraseology, was in a B-flat minor mode but lacked actual blues changes. Listening to it we are aware of a strong blues connotation and hot alto sax playing in the hard bop tradition and that ever-present freshness of line that McLean seemed to bring to standards and blues lines.

We know from Nat Hentoff's notes that he was, by this time, already involved with education and teaching in Harlem, with the youth band. As supervisor of HARYOU'S music department he was overseeing the eighteen-piece jazz band of this community action programme and was also developing classes in music theory, a choral workshop, a percussion division, a Latin band and a concert band. Jackie claimed that working with the kids enabled him to 'see the whole cycle of jazz – from the beginning to the outside we're now exploring.' He also claimed that it helped him with his own music. And he quoted a Charlie Parker memorial session at a club in Long Island where a good number of professional alto saxophonists played. 'But do you know who turned the place out?' he asked Hentoff. 'A sixteen-year-old youngster from HARYOU-ACT. These kids are something else.'

His own son Rene was in the HARYOU band at this time and his youngest, Vernon, was just about to join on trumpet. These were early days for McLean as jazz educator but with a full programme leading and recording with a regular quintet, teaching and encouraging his own sons to learn music, not to mention all the other young musicians and would-be musicians, his time must have been fully used up for most of his days and evenings. No time then for destructive pursuits like injecting heroin and although it must have been harrowingly difficult to get himself completely clean, the hard but satisfying regime of being a working musician, educator and family man, must have provided the stimulus to go through with it.

It has been pointed out, notably by Stephen H. Lehman in his article 'Jackie McLean as Improviser, Educator and Activist',[4] that McLean subsidised his earnings as a musician by teaching and taking part in programmes in inner city areas to help underprivileged youngsters. He spent five years with Robert Kennedy's Mobilization For Youth initiative and in the short film made about him in 1976, *Jackie McLean on Mars*, he said that this was something he had enjoyed: 'I worked with kids two or three afternoons a week and got a salary for it.' As Lehman puts it, it was another instance of McLean being able to respond 'constructively and resourcefully, to personal and professional challenges'. Because he responded to challenges in such a positive manner, he was able to work, educate and generally progress in his life without going into meltdown. This is, I feel, an important point, one that partly explains McLean's success story against all the odds, and his determination to succeed and keep his family intact throughout all the dark and harrowing times that heroin addiction had inflicted on him. We have only to look at Jackie's original inspiration on alto sax to see how easy it was to be drawn into a downward spiral where only the music survives.

So McLean continued to play in the clubs of NYC and Boston throughout 1964 and into 1965 and 1966. He was also still recording for Blue Note, the company that helped him to produce the finest of his recorded work for more than a decade. *Right Now* was the title of his next Blue Note LP, which he recorded on January 29th 1965 with a group comprising pianist Larry Willis, Bob Cranshaw on bass and Clifford Jarvis at the drums. Although he did not make many records as leader of a quartet, with no other front-line player, this setup seems to have suited him very well on the occasions he chose to use it and produce something special on disc. This recording is no exception.

No compromise here: from the opening two note phrase of 'Eco' the altoist is off on a typically charging, complex solo where his lyrically acidic lines are emotionally charged to such an extent that he always seems to be threatening to dissolve into chaos. He never does, of course, and that is why the best of McLean's solos are so engaging and worthy of constant, repeated study. This piece is modal although the bridge enters a different modal area with stop-time rhythm. Willis takes over from the leader and his supercharged piano solo maintains the level of intensity that Jackie has set up.

'Poor Eric' is a mournful requiem for Dolphy who had died a short time before. Playing the opening melody in unison with Cranshaw's arco bass was an inspired idea but the melancholy effect is almost unbearable to the sensitive listener. Jackie's heartfelt sorrow is adequately and unmistakably registered in a slow, powerfully expressed solo. Dolphy, a fellow alto sax master who was a leading figure in the free jazz movement for all too short a time, had died in a Berlin hospital when, possibly suffering from a rare blood disease and certainly in need of treatment, he was seen by nurses to be exhibiting what they interpreted, wrongly, as the effects of somebody strung out on heroin. Ironically and tragically because he never touched hard drugs, he was seen as an African-American jazz musician who must be strung out, and therefore left on a hospital bed to die. Knowing those facts, and we can be pretty sure that Jackie and the band did know, makes this sombre track all the more immediate and stark.

'Christel's Time' is a straight-ahead swinger with Jackie's charging solo relentlessly riding on the strong rhythmic carpet provided by Willis, Cranshaw and Jarvis. As Bob Blumenthal points out in his notes to the Van Gelder edition of this CD, Jackie's effortless flow on this track contains blues phrases in non-blues stretches and 'avant-garde sonic distortions onto the blues changes'. McLean was still building on his previous hard bop lineage but continually adding new methods of expressing himself.

'Right Now' has a bluesy, gospel feel in the piano chords provided by Willis but the headlong, supercharged solo by the leader leaves no doubt that he was in serious mood when he composed, played and, perhaps just as importantly, named this track. 'Right Now' came along at a time when McLean was busily aligning himself in the 'Freedom Now' movement and playing for civil rights organisations. Titles like *Action*, and *It's Time* all told the same story and left no doubt in anybody's mind where Jackie stood on civil rights. Titles like *Let Freedom Ring* however, had more double-edged intent. During an interview for public radio at the time, he told the interviewer that the album title *Let Freedom Ring* was intended to show the connection between the freedom demonstrated by creative improvisers and that sought by civil rights activists. As Steve Lehman pointed out in *Critical Studies in Improvisation*, by articulating his support for civil rights in this manner, McLean was aligning himself with people like Max Roach, Abbey Lincoln and Archie Shepp, who all used commercial recordings to advance political agendas. And although there is evidence that those three were restricted in their work opportunities for some time afterwards because of their fight for civil rights, the same unpleasant restrictions do not seem to have been applied to McLean.

During the 1960s he organised and performed benefit concerts regularly for the Black Panthers up and down the east coast of the USA. He also raised money for the Student Nonviolent Coordinating Committee (SNCC) and performed during the Newark riots in 1967. This commitment to the civil rights movement was maintained throughout the rest of his life. It is clear today that one of the reasons that McLean got into music education was his desire to improve the situation of African Americans in schools and community programmes. There was a groundswell of unrest at this time from black students with claims that jazz was being ignored in education and they wanted that situation addressed and changed. He would continue to work with the HARYOU-ACT programme during the early 1960s, along with the other initiatives, but his main interest was in playing as a professional jazz musician even though he was becoming increasingly unhappy with offers of work in clubs for exceedingly small amounts of money. He saw the move into education as a secondary occupation, one that would allow him to earn additional money and ensure that he did not have to accept offers if the money was unreasonably low.

Things were hotting up in the 1960s, in more ways than one. The events of that troubled decade were reflected far more accurately in the music of jazz soloists like McLean, Coltrane, Coleman and others than in the bleatings about all you need is love and flowers in your hair from the pop and rock singers of the time. Violence, change and unrest were all around with the political assassinations of President Kennedy, his brother Bobby, Martin Luther King and others, and the raging, spiralling Vietnam war; it was no wonder that, as Jackie said, the violence of the times was to be heard in the music.

16

NEW AND OLD GOSPEL

'My band made a transition in the '60s,' McLean told Ken Burns in his documentary *Jazz* in 1996. 'John F. Kennedy was blown away in 1963, Malcolm X, Medgar Evers, Martin Luther King, Robert Kennedy; all this assassination went on. The cities were burning. The civil rights movement was going on; people were screaming; the Vietnamese war. And so the music went that way.' These are Jackie's own words and they indicate strongly how he felt about things at the time, and also the reason his tone hardened up the way it did and the agitation that people heard in much of his music from this period. Like all the major improvising soloists in jazz, his tone did not appear fully formed one day and remain the same throughout his career. It changed frequently over the years as he and his music evolved and developed.

He continued to visit the recording studios regularly throughout 1965 although, once again, some of the recordings were not issued until several years later. A fairly large batch of unissued records from this period may be explained by the fact that Alfred Lion and Francis Wolff, the owners and shapers of Blue Note Records, were receiving offers to buy the company at this time and both admitted that, with the punishing schedule of recording and marketing the records, they were very tired and just about ready to sell up. They had received very low offers in the past which were not even considered but they finally sold the business to Liberty/United Artists in 1965. LP sessions which had been completed but had not received art work and catalogue numbers, remained on the shelves for several years.

On September 18th 1965, Jackie recorded under trumpeter Lee Morgan's leadership for his *Cornbread* LP. It was late coming out but it did at least receive a release within just over a year of completion. It is a sterling session with Morgan much more imaginative and inventive than usual and, of course, it benefits from the more free-thinking McLean contributions.

Six days later McLean went into the studio at Englewood Cliffs to record *Jacknife* with Charles Tolliver, Larry Willis, Larry Ridley on bass and Jack DeJohnette at the drums. It received a catalogue number, BLP 4223, but was not released until many years later on the LT series of reissues starting in 1978. There was another session for Lee Morgan in November 1965 which eventually came out as *Infinity* on the LT series and, in December of 1965, Jackie recorded *Consequence* with Lee Morgan on trumpet and Billy Higgins back on drums. Once again it was not released but, as became clear years later, there was nothing wrong with the music; it was just the sale of the Blue Note company that almost surely held up release of all this sterling material.

By March 1967, things were back to something like normal at the new Blue Note company and recordings were going ahead. One other first-rate session was shelved, inexplicably considering the quality of the music, was Jackie's *Hipnosis* where he teamed up again with trombonist Grachan Moncur and a tough rhythm section comprising Lamont Johnson on piano, Scotty Holt on bass and the ever-swinging, ever-reliable Billy Higgins on drums. Once again, this forward looking music which offered some of the very best of the avant-garde jazz of the time only came out on the LT reissue series in 1978, long after the first impact of this material could have been influential to young jazz musicians. The title track, 'Hipnosis', has a piano vamp all through as McLean and Moncur improvise some far-out solos although the music never strays enough from the conventional to lose any serious jazz enthusiast listeners. It would have impressed many young players, had they heard it, although it should be noted that the McLean group, usually with Tolliver, Lamont Johnson, Holt and Higgins or DeJohnette, could be heard in the clubs at this time.

One session that was quickly released, and could hardly have failed to stir up interest and curiosity, was the meeting of McLean and Ornette Coleman on the LP *New and Old Gospel* (BST 84262). It must have appealed strongly to Jackie who was always interested in mixing styles or eliminating style divisions completely where possible. Here was his chance to record with the man who had inspired him to seek new avenues of expression. McLean had declared to Spellman that he regarded Lester Young as a bebop player and said that he thought that when Lester was away from the Basie rhythm section and played with Big Sid Catlett behind him 'he got a different type of swing'. McLean thought of Catlett as an early bop drummer. I can't escape the thought that Jackie possibly felt that working with Ornette would somehow similarly elevate him completely into the realm of an avant-garde jazzman, at least at that time and in the mood he was then in.

This could have been a monumental session with two of the most inventive and intuitive alto saxophonists in jazz, shaping up and swapping lines together in friendly but competitive mode. I cannot help but regard it as the missed opportunity of the decade, perhaps even the century, when it was decided, mutually it seems, that Ornette would play trumpet. LP liner note writer Nat Hentoff stated that Coleman was prepared to play any of his instruments but it seemed to Jackie that they would best complement each other if Ornette focused on trumpet. Communications between the two musicians were good: 'You know, we had never played together before, but once we got started, there were no problems.'

Coleman agreed and added, 'I hadn't expected any. I love the way Jackie plays and the way he writes. He's such a beautiful musician. And so it was a very good, happy session.' Maybe and yet I can't stop the thought that it could have been so much better. It was, after all, Coleman whose new music had inspired Jackie to play in a much freer manner from 1962 onwards, as he himself pointed out in his liner notes to *Let Freedom Ring*. With McLean, arguably the most important bop soloist on alto after Charlie Parker, playing together with the father of free jazz on the instrument, duetting, sparring, driving each other on, what could we have expected from a two alto album?

One important musician was in no doubt about how wrong the choice of instrument for Ornette was. In his notes for the 2006 Rudy Van Gelder edition of this CD, Bob Blumenthal talks of meeting pianist Cecil Taylor in 1968, shortly after this session was recorded. Taylor told him that he had been approached to play piano on the record but had declined. He told Blumenthal that he had nothing but admiration for McLean's work, but could not endorse public performance on an instrument without years of preparation, as Coleman, on trumpet, was about to do. Somewhat over the top perhaps, but then Taylor was and is a no-compromise musician and he must have felt sufficiently correct about his decision to pass up the opportunity of a recording session with two other major soloists in 1967. In those early days of free jazz activity, record sessions were not easy to come by for any member of the avant-garde and Taylor had not reached anywhere near the level of eminence as a musician that he enjoys today.

Speculating on what could have been is an intriguing but ultimately useless and time-wasting exercise. What we actually got was a fascinating quintet where McLean's rich, acidic alto swapped choruses with the tentative, often lightweight but certainly unique trumpet stylings of Coleman. The first half of the original LP release is taken up by a McLean composition in four parts, 'Lifeline'. It was intended to represent a complete life experience 'from birth to death' in Jackie's words. From

'Offspring' to the final 'The Inevitable End' we hear various interpretations of life through the instruments with McLean passionate and intense through most sections and Ornette often sounding quite frantic but, it has to be said, like no other trumpet player before or since. On the slow passages of this piece his trumpet is full of strained melancholy and, although his tone is weak, the personal sound comes through. It may not match or come anywhere near his alto saxophone stylings but it is undeniable that Coleman's improvised lines and sound have their own personal resonance. He is a completely original, free spirit who always plays instinctively as he feels at the moment. If he lacks certain technical facilities or is not as polished in performance as some of his contemporaries, he more than compensates with the breadth of his imagination and the freshness and originality of his lines.

This is McLean's date, he is the leader and he plays very well in his usual manner for this period of his career. But it is Coleman who grabs the attention time and again with the sheer freshness of his conception and the way his trumpet playing sounds different from any earlier attempts on this instrument. The effect on McLean is to stimulate him to play in a looser, more adventurous manner on this session. Always open to learn, and having credited Coleman with inspiring him to a new and more contemporary style of playing, he frequently gets caught up here in responding to Coleman's lines with more adventurous forays of his own.

'Old Gospel' was written for the date by Coleman and it shows a love of old style gospel music with a buoyant lift from the section. 'This has a real old time churchy feeling,' Jackie says in the liner and goes on to assert that, although some people might be surprised that it came from Ornette, he knew it was there, deep down inside him, 'all the time'. It is a surprise on first hearing, to find the opening theme statement and the quintet sounding like Art Blakey and the Jazz Messengers but only Lamont

Johnson's piano solo continues in that manner. Jackie's alto is intense and and his inventive solo is punctuated with jagged cries and that high-pitched scream he used first on *Let Freedom Ring*. Coleman manages to produce a much more earthy trumpet sound here and, in spite of Cecil Taylor's comments, I think he had a pretty good working knowledge of the instrument at this time. 'Old Gospel' is still, ultimately, a soul and blues-type romp with all its avant-garde trappings.

The final selection, 'Strange as it Seems', finds Jackie stating the melody as Ornette weaves around him on trumpet – in a different tempo, 'a free tempo' as he put it. This is a much darker composition and the solos are heavy with lurking menace. Coleman described it as a 'combination of elements which are quite different from each other but at the same time are involved in a deep relationship'. Coleman, muted, traces a sombre, menacing solo sequence and, following him, Johnson's trenchant chords hardly relieve the atmospheric doom. Although their tasks are confined to providing a rhythmic backing without soloing, Scotty Holt and Billy Higgins offer sympathetic support throughout and by doing so throw into relief the forceful, burgeoning solos of the two principals.

The record may not be counted as one of their favourites by many McLean or Coleman followers but it was a disc that had to be made and it is valuable for showing us how two major soloists responded to each other musically. They were compatible, as the three extended tracks demonstrate, and although Coleman is the more important figure in terms of innovation, both were major modern jazz soloists with different approaches but many facets in common. What a shame that they never locked alto saxophones together.

17

TEACHING

Jackie McLean made his first ventures into teaching in the 1960s although, at this time, it was very much as an addition to his profession as a working jazz musician. His early work, after leaving the cast of *The Connection* back in 1961, was primarily with HARYOU-ACT in New York City and functioning as a bandmaster in a penitentiary. This last may have been occasioned to some extent by his wishing to help young people in that situation because he himself had seen the inside of a prison cell on several occasions for drug related offences. The most recent incarceration had been in 1964, the year he decided to shake off the drug addiction forever.

Once clean himself and knowing from long, bitter experience, the damage that hard drugs, heroin in particular, could do, he was in a position to function as a drug counsellor to help others. This work was also a positive response to a new challenge, the first of many to come.

In 1968 McLean began his association with the University of Hartford. Although he was working as a drug counsellor, he was soon approached by students who were dissatisfied with the school's 'Eurocentric music curriculum'. Soon afterwards he began teaching classes in music history and improvisation. It was all part of the black student activist movement of the late 1960s; in response to the demand for black studies curricula, many of the leading American universities, Hartford included, began to hire African-American artists, musicians and scholars in large numbers. Jazz musicians who made early moves into academia were those who had already demonstrated a commitment to community activism and the civil rights movement. Tenor saxophonist Archie Shepp was another improvising jazz musician who found a place as an educator at a university, in his case in Buffalo.

McLean became part of the music faculty of the university's Hartt School in 1970. Although he already had five years experience in NYC as a teacher, he reported feeling most ill-prepared to teach at university level. In the same year Jackie was interviewed for a programme called *Jazz Portraits* on US radio station WGBH 89.7, and told the interviewer that he had said to the Hartford faculty, 'Look, I don't know anything about anything except what I experienced.' He said that he also talked to other musicians at this time and they told him that his experiences were exactly what the university was hiring him for. 'They don't expect you to talk about ragtime and all that; go with what you know,' he was told. According to Steve Lehman,[1] McLean's early teaching classes relied heavily on his close association with major jazz soloists and his own experiences working with them and as a leader himself. But, being as thorough and determined as ever to get everything he did absolutely right, he decided to acquire a much more comprehensive knowledge of African-American jazz. By the early 1970s he had studied the lives and music of Fats Waller and Jelly Roll Morton for starters.

As he told the interviewer on *Jazz Portraits*: 'I remember thinking that it won't be bad if I find out what came before me. And maybe I need to find that out. And I was very happy that I did because what came before really made my musical style mellow and blossom and it made me more comfortable, and it really pointed to where I should go.'

Jackie certainly seems to have adapted well to teaching from the very beginning and his comments at this time all indicate that he considered it something that would aid his progress as an improvising musician, on the one hand, and give him a measure of security, on the other. He was very scathing about having had to accept playing jobs for very low, almost insulting fees in the past, fees that were never worthy of a major soloist and improvising musician with a good name and reputation. Jazz musicians have always had to accept low pay and poor treatment from promoters and concert halls and, as an educator with a separate source of income, he felt that he no longer had to accept these insults.

In the film *Jackie McLean on Mars*[2] he talked about employment as a musician in the 1950s and the '60s. And it was just the same in the 1970s, he claimed. 'When you're not playing you got to worry about how you're going to pay your bills and a lot of things.' He said that he didn't want to go through that again and he saw a little security at the university. Understandable enough given the scuffling for work and not getting paid a living wage for it but McLean was quick to point out that he just wanted to get out of playing every night and, these are the crucial words: '*I wanted to go somewhere where I could perpetuate some concepts from another vantage point and not just on the bandstand.*' So he made it clear that there was always a double purpose in pursuing a career in education: he wanted to study his craft from a different angle and in so doing pass on his considerable knowledge to his students and, at the same time, to acquire a certain amount of financial security.

Jackie instructed his students through meticulously organised lectures spiced up with personal reminiscences and tales of the jazz life as he had known it and lived it. His anecdotes were always interesting and his experiences of working with almost all of the major jazz figures of the time must have impressed and inspired his students. Close contact and playing with Charlie Parker, Miles Davis, Charles Mingus and Art Blakey, to name only a few, provided many a fascinating story for his classrooms. And, as he had said to Spellman shortly before taking up his long-term teaching post in Hartford, he was mainly concerned with sound. 'It's not about notation really,' he said and went on to suggest that he could write down every chord and dissonance that Thelonious Monk played, then play it back and, 'then it wouldn't be Monk.' McLean's concern with getting a strong, identifiable personal sound from an instrument is something he is likely to have stressed to all his students in the early years.

Talking to Ken Burns in 1996, Jackie told him that the music of that day was still reflecting what was going on in the world. 'And environment, you know, and what we live in, you know? And right now, if you listen to the music now, you're hearing this whole period of violence getting ready to erupt, and I don't know where it's going to show.' He went on to say that the music he played was still moving along in one particular direction, following the concepts of 'Duke Ellington and Louis Armstrong and all these great men who have set this direction for us. You know we already have our road kind of mapped out for us. It will change.... Young musicians will bring other ideas, rhythms will change and concepts will change but this music is always ever developing and ever moving on, you know?'[3]

Questioned about fusion he was much more cautious but said that he liked some of Miles Davis' later music. While he admitted to disagreement with some of the statements Miles made, McLean told Burns that he never disagreed with any sound that came out of Miles' trumpet. When asked about the opinion of many jazz enthusiasts that the musicians coming up were sounding very academic, he did not agree. He felt that the music had gone through very many changes from ragtime to big band to bop to free style, and that young musicians had reexamined the music, and had looked again at Coltrane. He concluded by saying: 'I think the music is in very good hands.'

Coming from somebody who, at the time he was interviewed by Burns in 1994, had spent many years teaching young students and researching the roots of jazz and the early pioneers, this represents, it seems to me, a positive optimism that should help to reassure all those many people who insist that jazz is dying or doomed to eventual obscurity. It has a habit of going in and out of fashion and being more popular in some decades than others but the music has developed and matured at an alarming rate in a short span of a hundred years and it always bounces back at the precise moment that the pessimists declare it dead and buried.

McLean spent many years studying the music from the early days during slavery and right through to modern times so it was not just a case of a cursory study of a few key early soloists but, as Dollie McLean told me, a thorough investigation in depth. Although Jackie declared in *Jackie McLean on Mars* that he had felt like a poor exploited musician in 1966, he was able to add in the next sentence: 'And I also feel like a professor of music history at the University of Hartford.' It indicates clearly how important the teaching was to him and how it must have helped him to develop as a musician and major soloist without the unacceptable pressures of being a jazz musician knowing his own worth but constantly being exploited and underpaid.

When Jackie and Dollie founded the Hartt School of Jazz, which later came to be named the 'Jackie McLean Institute of Jazz', the programme focused on jazz and African-American idioms and included special courses on improvisation, music history, jazz transcriptions and arranging. Students were given the opportunity to perform regularly throughout their undergraduate careers. Because of Jackie's reputation as an improvising soloist and a major jazz leader he was able to bring top names to the school to instruct, interact and play music with the students. Eddie Henderson the trumpet player and Max Roach, one of the pioneering bebop drummers, were early visitors. Others who played and instructed over the years include Milt Jackson, Wynton Marsalis, Dizzy Gillespie, Ahmad Jamal, and Art Blakey and his Messengers.

His work at the university and his own position there might

not have amounted to much more than a token appointment that did not last long had he not worked tirelessly in the early years to establish himself and the music he represented. The first task he set himself was to get African-American jazz on the agenda and treated, as it should have been from the outset, as serious, important music. In 1968, at the University of Hartford, African-American music was not treated with anything like the respect that Western European classical music was. He stated in *Jackie McLean on Mars* that terms like 'legitimate music' and 'serious music' were constantly used in conversation, implying that music that did not fit those categories was not serious or indeed legitimate. 'So I have used that term,' Jackie said. 'What they call "jazz", I call that a classical music. It's an American classical music.'

McLean worked hard through the 1970s to secure his position as a permanent faculty member and established the first university department of African-American music at Hartford by the middle of that decade. He brought in pianist/composer Jackie Byard and saxophonist/composer Paul Jeffrey as additional faculty members and in due course he was even able to make his department into a degree-granting entity.[4] His appointment, it was soon evident, was no token post that would terminate in two or three years and be forgotten; this was the real thing and Jackie's abilities as a teacher and lecturer would flourish as he sought to provide a solid base of technical knowledge, liberally laced with anecdotes and personal experiences from around twenty years experience as a working jazz musician. All those years of discussion and early study with Bud Powell, the gigs heard and later shared with Charlie Parker, the work in the studios and on the road with the likes of Miles Davis, Art Blakey's Messengers and Charles Mingus would have been invaluable. And there is evidence that McLean used all of those experiences, and his own as a leader from around 1958 onwards, in helping to formulate his teaching programmes at Hartford.

'He was a wonderful story teller,' Dollie McLean told me as

she regretted that he had not had time to complete his autobiography. A great communicator, talker, raconteur and someone with an ability to reach out to people, all these qualities would have helped him in what must initially have been a difficult task: the establishment, on a permanent basis, of the Hartt School's jazz programme. He also appears to have been very popular with the students, with many of them anxious to get time with him to discuss their personal theories or hang-ups. A former student, Paul Berliner, in his book *Thinking in Jazz*, reported that one student, explaining why he valued McLean's words and tuition so highly said: 'It had to do with his personality. – He was always so positive that just to have a word from him was enough to send me home to practice for hours. It was enough to keep me going until the next time I saw him again.'

Jackie McLean, jazz saxophonist, composer and bandleader, was now able to add 'successful university professor' to his list of accomplishments although, at the time, what he was really achieving in that way probably never crossed his mind.

18

MUSICIAN, SOLOIST, EDUCATOR AND ACTIVIST

Jackie kept busy in the recording studios throughout 1967 and only began to slow down in 1968. The *Hipnosis* session which included his old friend Grachan Moncur came first on February 3rd 1967, and this was one of his best LPs of the late 1960s, making it all the more inexplicable that it did not get a release at the time. Then, on February 15th, he recorded two tracks on a compilation, *Tribute to Charlie Parker*, issued by RCA Victor (LPM 3783). On March 24th he recorded the session with Ornette Coleman and, in September of that year, *'Bout Soul* where he was reunited with Moncur, and Rashied Ali came in on drums.

On September 22nd Jackie found himself in the Van Gelder studios with old pal Lee Morgan on trumpet for a Blue Note record under the leadership of pianist Jack Wilson. The pianist was not very well-known at this time and has hardly made much of a name for himself in jazz although this session comes across as a fairly typical Blue Note date of the time. It starts off with 'Do It' – a funky blues in the 'Sidewinder' style that most Blue Note dates were required to feature after Lee Morgan's unexpected success with his disc in 1964. Blue Note had by this time been sold to Liberty Records and pianist Duke Jordan came in to produce this one.

Things were changing and in a few years time Blue Note Records would be a different proposition from the company that Alfred Lion and Francis Wolff nurtured from 1939 to 1965.

This 1967 session is still very much in the old Blue Note style but Wilson was not a typical Blue Note pianist. The record works because of the sterling solos by Morgan and McLean, old sparring partners and hard bop soloists of the front rank from way back. Along with two first class rhythm section men in Bob Cranshaw and Billy Higgins, they lift this session to the height of a typical Blue Note date and that in itself is quite an accomplishment. The other point to bear in mind here is that by the time this set was recorded McLean had been working and recording in a much more free jazz style and extending his own and other musicians' boundaries. This session however is something of a throwback to the old hard bop and blues days of the late 1950s and the early 1960s. Jackie happily joins forces with Morgan and trombonist Garnett Brown and turns in free flowing but hardly avant-garde solos as he reaches back to the days when this style was the one he played all the time. If nothing else, it demonstrates yet again that his mind was constantly open and that he was as happy in the old as he was in the new. Perhaps the hard bop, surely the most consistent, durable and longest lasting of all jazz styles, was still his greatest musical love and there is much evidence to support the theory that it remained his overall favourite means of musical expression until the day he died.

A couple of weeks after the Wilson session, Jackie was back at Van Gelder's studio to record *Hi Voltage* for leader and old friend Hank Mobley. This was, in many ways, even more of a throwback to the old style with Hank programming a soul-type blues, 'High Voltage', to begin the disc and following up with 'Bossa De Luxe' and 'Flirty Girty'. The latter is a slow, funky blues of the kind that both Jackie and Hank used to play regularly and you can hear clearly in the playing that they are both enjoying themselves immensely. Mobley's solo sails out of the ensemble with plenty of warmth of expression and is followed by a bright, extrovert trumpet segment from Blue Mitchell. Jackie is intense, emotionally charged, as he was on almost everything he played, but there is still that underlying feeling of having fun with the slight theme which runs right through the disc. Dollie McLean told me that he and Mobley were good friends and Jackie respected Hank as a musician. That certainly shows through on every track here.

The feverish recording activity continued just one month later when, on November 10th, Jackie again joined with Lee Morgan for the trumpeter's *The Sixth Sense* (Blue Note BST 84335), another fiery session in the advanced hard bop manner. Players like Morgan were never content to coast on what they had done in the past and he had proved with his *Cornbread* release that his music was changing and moving forward. McLean had been a first choice, important contributor to that disc as well. Morgan's writing on the first three tracks of this set shows that he is moving out into a freer sense and style of playing and the ensemble writing for the sextet is impressive. McLean would have recognised this as a typical bop blowing date of the day with contemporary flourishes and thoroughly approved of it even if, on his own discs of the time, he was searching out means of expression and methods of writing and playing that were considerably different.

It was the calm before the storm: a hectic flourish of recording activity in which everybody worked in their usual enthusiastic, creative manner just before everything blew up in their faces and Blue Note Records axed their major recording soloists and began to pursue more actively the soul/pop/R&B music that they saw as a means of making their fortunes. Blue Note under the Liberty Records banner was not the company it had been; Lion and Wolff loved the music and that came first, even if they lost money on promoting a particularly good but not very commercial musician, which they frequently did. The new owners were far more commercially minded and, presumably, could see the way things were going as early as 1967. Rock and pop records were becoming ever more popular and selling in huge numbers, whether it was the Beatles or a relatively unknown singer with a guitar who could only play two chords. Miles Davis was beginning to move away from straight-ahead jazz with *Nefertiti* in 1967, the first indication of a radical change in his music, although it was his *Bitches Brew*, two years later, that set off rock or pop jazz.

Things were changing rapidly. Jackie recorded *Demon's Dance* for Blue Note (BST 84345) on December 22nd 1967 with his regulars of the time: Woody Shaw on trumpet, Lamont Johnson, piano, Scotty Holt, bass, and Jack DeJohnette at the drums. It was not one of his better records but it proved to be the last for that company in that decade. A sextet date on July 5th 1968 at Plaza Sound studios, in itself a complete break with tradition and Blue Note practice, recorded five tracks that were rejected by the company. Bobby Hutcherson was back on vibes, Tyrone Washington came in on tenor sax and Woody Shaw was on trumpet so it is strange to see that none of the material recorded was considered suitable for issue by Blue Note. Or maybe it was a far-out session that Blue Note, under the influence of their new masters, considered unsuitable and not in keeping with their plans for the company in the next decade.

Their plans for this famous jazz label with its illustrious history turned out to involve severing links with all the major soloists who had given it its reputation over the past twenty years except for pianist Horace Silver who stayed on until the mid-1980s. Not that he produced anything of lasting value after 1967 that I am aware of.

There had been, however, a feverish amount of recording going on at Blue Note between 1965 and 1968. A McLean session from December 1965 called *Consequence* was not released in that decade but, like so many others, came out on an LT series release in 1979 (Blue Note LT 99). Then there was another session from April 1966 called *High Frequency* which, although it was given a catalogue number (BLP 4236), eventually appeared in 1975 as part of the double LP *Jacknife* (BLP LA457 H2), together with five tracks from September 1965.

Jacknife is a curious case. Following the 1970s release on LP the 1965 tracks were eventually put out on a limited edition CD in 2002 as Blue Note 40532 but the *High Frequency* tracks have never been released as a separate record. Of the 1965 tracks, 'On the Nile' finds Jackie in a Coltrane bag producing furiously percussive notes at white hot intensity in a long, convoluted modal piece which is stoked up and nurtured by Larry Willis at the piano, Larry Ridley, bass, and Jack DeJohnette at the drum kit. Unusually, Jackie had both his current trumpeter, Charles Tolliver, and old buddy Lee Morgan on hand. Tolliver delivers a scorching solo on this track, as intense as the leader's contribution and it is only Willis' gentler, lyrical intervention, at the end of the trumpet solo, that brings the selection down to a softer, more lyrical workout. In fact Willis' rhapsodic solo almost changes the direction of the piece completely as Ridley follows him with a short, thoughtful solo segment. When the horns return at the end they are less aggressive and assertive but seemingly happy to end the track on a melodic reiteration of the theme.

'Climax', which follows, is a swinger employing stop time devices. Jackie is hard-swinging and passion-filled as always and his solo lines more in the hard bop bag than the opening selection. At this time, in particular, he was never sure which direction he wanted to take on records so he hedged his bets by offering a freestyle solo on the opener, as here, followed by a hard bop outing on the next. The presence on this track of Morgan, rather than Tolliver, may also have coloured his decision to go with the old rather than the new. And Jackie never went all out in an effort to change and move on, as for example Coltrane did; with him it was always a case of augmenting what he knew and loved with new, often progressive, sometimes radical, ideas.

That is why McLean's music, down through the years, has always been easy for bop enthusiasts to assimilate.

'Soft Blue' is perhaps the most attractive track with solos from Morgan the composer, Tolliver and the leader showing a warm affection for the blues with a pulsating solo that registers joy above all other emotions. Tolliver's solo is strong and well structured but he can't match the invention and technical resource of Morgan on this one. What we end up with here is a good, all round McLean Blue Note session of the day, bright, full of inspired solo work from him and his sidemen and brisk, inspired rhythm section work.

Jackie's last issued Blue Note, under the old company, was *Demon's Dance* from December 1967 and after that there appears to be a gap of five years where no commercial recordings were made. This is not in any way surprising as setting up his new job and a fresh home in Hartford would have occupied a lot of time, followed by his settling in as a successful lecturer and educator.

In his teaching, once he had established himself and begun to work out presentation patterns and methods, he started to look at how and why the music was moving in the direction it was at that time. He worked out lessons to show how what was going on in the community influenced the musicians and the music, although some of his students were baffled at first. When he introduced a lecture on the death of President John F. Kennedy a student raised his hand and asked what relevance this had to the subject matter.[1] Jackie responded: 'I explained to him that the government and what it perpetuates is a reflection of what the art form is.' He went on to add that surely in Nazi Germany they didn't have any John Coltranes because they outlawed certain art forms and burned certain books. 'And I saw the death of John F. Kennedy as being very relevant to where the art was going in this country.'

McLean was ahead of his time in many of his teaching methods as described by Steve Lehman,[2] his own recollections on radio and in *Jackie McLean on Mars*. He allied himself closely to the Black Panther movement and other freedom fighting units, taught the history of African-American culture and its music and the interaction of all the different threads. It must have been exhilarating for many students, if baffling for a few, to learn not just about the music they loved but the history of that music and the people who made it from earliest times to the present day.

When Jackie and Dollie set up the Artists Collective in 1970, he was working full-time as a lecturer at the University of Hartford. They set up the collective in a poor area in order to draw in youngsters who perhaps would not have ventured near, nor had a chance to take part, had it been in an up-market residential neighbourhood. This was a conscious decision to draw in under-privileged youngsters. Jackie said at the time that he and Dollie wanted to build a music and cultural centre that would be possible here but fairly unlikely to get off the ground in New York City. 'I remember thinking,' he said, 'in New York City there's a thousand Dollie McLeans and a million Jackie McLeans but in Hartford perhaps we can do something we couldn't do so readily in New York and that is build a cultural centre.'[3]

With his status at the time as a top-drawer soloist and bandleader, it would have been all too easy and, almost certainly, far more financially rewarding to have set up his collective in a residential suburb. That, of course, was not what McLean was about; from the earliest days he had recorded and often worked with young musicians, including many from under-privileged backgrounds, giving them a chance to establish themselves, and he continued this policy right to the end of his life. After the Artists Collective had become established, his recordings featured students he had trained, including some whose education was complete and were working professionally, but many who were still learning. In a radio interview, *Jazz Portraits*, he made the point that it would be much easier for him to get five experienced musicians, people like Cedar Walton and Billy Higgins, and go out and play. Then he wouldn't need to worry at all about what might happen, what might go wrong. 'But,' he said, 'I like young musicians, because they make mistakes and they cause things to happen on the stage. And then we straighten it out and move forward.' Most telling of all was his last sentence: 'And at the same time, little new things slip in here and there through these encounters.'

Jackie never ever lost an opportunity to improvise and turn this to advantage, not only in music but on the stage as well, making the most of whatever happened there and using it creatively and intelligently. It must have been hazardous at times but how much more satisfying, creating new and fresh music with young players rather than going through the motions to some extent with seasoned veterans who knew, almost before he did, what he was going to play next.

* * *

The success story of Jackie McLean as educator for something over thirty years is almost unique. His achievement, in persuading a conservative university to start a long-term programme to educate students in the field of African-American jazz, was considerable. When I spoke to Dollie McLean, I asked her how it had all started; how had he come to start teaching in the first place at a prestigious university? She told me that he was asked to come and teach in Hartford by a young student who was studying double bass. The young man approached him at a gig at Slugs club in NYC where Jackie was playing with his combo. He must have been pretty persuasive because McLean made approaches to the Hartt School and was invited, in due course, to become artist in residence. Once he had begun he soon collected further requests to teach the students and began to look closely at the set-up at the university.

'There was no music of any other kind except classical,' said Dollie McLean. Studies of African-American music and culture were unheard of at that time and place. So Jackie set about persuading, cajoling and perhaps even attempting to bully the authorities into letting him start a regular class. Eventually they gave him what he and many students wanted and, although several similar programmes followed at other universities in due course, most of them lasted only a year or two or fizzled out for lack of support and nourishment. Indeed, only the seminal Association for the Advancement of Creative Musicians and the Artists Collective have survived from the 1970s until the present day and are still flourishing.

19

THE ARTISTS COLLECTIVE

What started in 1970 as a new, ambitious and hopeful project in backstreet rooms and students' quarters is today a thriving establishment. It boasts, accurately, that it is the only multi-arts and cultural organisation of its kind in Connecticut 'emphasising the cultural and artistic contributions of the African Diaspora'. The Artists Collective website lists Jackie McLean as founder and Dollie McLean as 'founding executive director', a post she occupies at the time of writing. The McLean's daughter Melonae, involved over the years in popular music and radio, now works regularly on the administrative side of the Collective. Their elder son Rene often played with his father and became the director of the big band that Jackie used to run. He is also a major saxophonist and flautist who held a post as a lecturer in jazz studies at the University of Cape Town before returning home.

When I first tried to make contact with Dollie, I felt for a long time that it was not going to be easy and in fact it took several email exchanges and about three months before I heard from her. As soon as I read the opening paragraph of her reply I understood. She apologised for the long delay but confessed that she was 'still dealing with Jackie's leaving and finding it difficult to do all of what needs to be done and ensuring his legacy.' I realised that I should have been aware of her closeness to her late husband; after all they had been together since the early days in New York when they went out along with Charlie Parker, the two alto men often sharing a hired saxophone and, on occasions, a shared gig. A marriage that had lasted that long, a couple that lived together for all those years, would make the departure of one hard to bear for the surviving partner. She told me that he had been writing his autobiography but sadly had not had time to complete it. Dollie now wants to complete it with help from family members or close friends and it is to be hoped that she does, for all and any writings by this important and unique jazz musician should be welcome indeed. Especially welcome would be further insight into Jackie's home life, something that outsiders can only cover in relative brevity, as well as more on his approach to his professional activities.

Dollie emphasised that Jackie spent many years researching the evolution and development of jazz. He was a great talker, she said, 'with lots of humour and insight when talking about many of his personal experiences and his life in general.' In conversation with American writer Ben Sidran some years ago, McLean talked about the strength of his and Dollie's commitment to the Collective, 'I find that most of the strides that Dollie and I have made have been shooting from the hip and keeping our dream in front of us and not wavering from it. It's been very helpful improvising.'

Initially the intention may have been a desire to steer youngsters away from bad things, as Jackie himself put it during his radio interview *Jazz Portraits*: 'to provide a place where kids can grow up and have a good time.' He wanted to steer them away from narcotics, drinking and early pregnancy; problems that, then as now, are the root cause of much distress for young people and their families. Somehow though, it just grew and grew. Dance and drama were soon added to music, and teaching staff appointed.

Although the Artists Collective started off by holding its first classes in borrowed spaces throughout the city, a beautiful three-storey schoolhouse built in the 1920s became its new home in 1975 through the courtesy of the City of Hartford. Large-scale concerts, gospel music, student showcases and special theatrical and dance presentations are still put on in rented venues throughout the city.

More recently, the Artists Collective moved into a brand new, specially designed modern building at 1200 Albany Avenue in the city centre, described on its website as 'a key component of the economic development of the city of Hartford and the North Hartford Albany Avenue corridor'.

All this would not have been possible, of course, without constant hard work, struggle and determination on the part of Jackie and Dollie McLean through those crucial, early years. Hardest of all was the establishment of a class to teach jazz on a permanent basis at the university, one that like the others in the USA at that time did not consider jazz as a serious music. So busy were the McLeans in those first four years that Jackie did not record and it is unlikely that he played many live gigs. By August 1972, however, he was able to travel to Europe and he recorded at the Jazzhus Montmartre in Copenhagen. Fellow American Kenny Drew was there on piano while the rhythm team were Europeans: bassist Bo Stief and drummer Alex Riel. He continued to work and record in Denmark from 1972 to '74 and at one point linked up with tenor saxophonist Dexter Gordon, an old friend from his New York days. In October 1974 he was in New York City although still being recorded by Danish record company, Steeplechase.

In 1976, Jackie teamed up again with Mal Waldron for a tour of Japan and they recorded for Japanese Victor in Tokyo on April 12th. A firm favourite after 1962, drummer Billy Higgins was back on drums and they employed Japanese bassist Isao Susuki. By this time McLean had started to work again fairly consistently but there were long periods, as his work at Hartford University and the Artists Collective built up, when he found it difficult even to practise regularly, never mind take gigs or recording dates.

'It is a serious sacrifice,' he complained in the film *Jackie McLean on Mars*, 'but at this point I don't get a chance to practise.' He went on to say that he did not have the energy to practise after covering the many things he had to do in a day and added that it was a problem he was constantly fighting. He would promise himself, after playing a gig and reaching a certain point in his playing, that once he returned to Hartford he would set aside at least an hour every day to practise and keep in shape. It never happened. He confessed that on return from gigs a day went by, then a week, and he ended up getting back into the usual rigorous work routine and not getting around to practising. He also talked about the effect this had on his lips and breathing when he did try to play after a long layoff caused by other work.

Striking a balance between creative playing, teaching and lecturing and maintaining a regular practice schedule became impossible, as it had for many others in Jackie's position, and it must be admitted that some of those people had fallen by the wayside or had their teaching posts curtailed because they were not producing the required results.

By the time he had been working at the university and the Collective for twenty years, Jackie McLean had been looking for a way to slow down or retire from the arduous workload he had built up. But he couldn't do it. In *Jazz Portraits* he told the interviewer, 'I keep saying, "This is it. When this kid graduates I'm finished." And I come in September and here's some little kid that can play so great. And I say, "Maybe I can do four more years and get him out of here." Because when I see them arrive I don't want to leave them. I want to help them and see where they can go.'

Retiring from work that was so satisfying and worthwhile was never going to be a realistic option for Jackie and he must soon have realised it.

For many of his students, the methods used by McLean as a saxophonist and improvising musician were passed on and by using these they were able to forge distinctive styles and sounds of their own in due course. Saxophonists like Jimmy Greene, Mike DiRubbo, Wayne Escoffery, Kris Allen, Steve Lehmann, and Abraham Burton all benefited considerably by attending McLean's classes. Burton in particular has a hard, strident alto tone that sounds very much like his teacher's later sound although he still retains his own unique quality of phrasing and presentation. There are occasions on records though where Burton sounds more like Jay Mac than McLean himself.

As the years went by at Hartford, McLean began to develop various new techniques of playing. He came up with what Lehman described as 'personal improvisatory strategies, which he referred to as "systems".' His music became more and more personal and unique, reversing the almost universal strategy of playing only what you know: music that was studied and developed in youth and only slightly refined in later years. And Jackie never kept anything to himself. Whatever new methods he developed he passed on to his students. Many were so anxious to emulate everything he taught them that they tried to play just like him, something he frequently had to discourage in some of the alto saxophonists. One unnamed student even had a reprimand from McLean for sounding too much like his teacher that he took as a compliment!

There is also evidence, left on recordings, that Jackie found the teaching of young students a two-way exercise; his own playing reflected some of the phrasing and little licks that young players used at that time. His son Rene played in his father's combo frequently throughout the late 1980s and early 1990s: 'It was my most rewarding, my most exciting and my most challenging experience,' Rene said about working with his father. 'I had to rise to the occasion. It made no difference if I was his son or his brother.' He also said that they had many magical musical moments together and 'Many times we could finish each other's ideas. It was just unique and mystical.'[1]

The affinity between two very accomplished musicians who are also father and son might be expected to produce startling results but there are also many examples of McLean's students claiming that he inspired them to great musical heights. Whatever the magic was, Jackie McLean continued to sprinkle it over students from 1970 until his death in March 2006.

20

LATE FLOURISHES

Although there was a break in recording activity between 1967 and 1972, McLean continued from then on and eventually returned to a pretty full schedule of performing in public and recording. In August 1972 he was recording in Copenhagen and then linked with Gary Bartz and Charlie Mariano for another Danish recording in 1973 and, in the same year back at the Jazzhus Montmartre, he played with Kenny Drew, bassist Niels-Henning Ørsted Pedersen and drummer Alex Riel. While playing at that famous venue, he worked and recorded with tenor saxophonist Dexter Gordon, one of Jackie's idols from the early days in Sugar Hill. So, by this time, he was back combining a full workload, touring, playing and recording, with his new and important duties in Hartford. Little wonder that he found no time for practising!

By October 1974 back in NYC he recorded with drummer/percussionist Michael Garvin in a duo setting for Steeplechase. At the same session, he also recorded with a sextet that included his son Rene on tenor sax.

There was a recording issued in 1978 with Hank Jones, Ron Carter on bass and Tony Williams, which was billed as the Great Jazz Trio. Then, after a gap of a few years when, no doubt, he was busy teaching at Hartford, there was a brief return to the new Blue Note company where he recorded as part of the *One Night with Blue Note* sessions at the Town Hall in NYC with Woody Shaw on trumpet and McCoy Tyner on piano. There was also a studio session with Tyner for Blue Note, but these were isolated instances as the company had changed considerably, concentrating now more than ever on soul and rhythm and blues music with jazz very much a sideline.

In 1986 he toured Japan again and recorded there with a line-up including Mal Waldron, his almost constant piano companion in the 1950s, and Herbie Lewis, the bassist from his *Let Freedom Ring* set in 1962. Then, in 1988, things started to change quite dramatically when Jackie began to perform in public and record with some of his students, including his son Rene. The first disc was *Dynasty* by the McLean Quintet, (Triloka 181-2) recorded live in Hollywood, California, in front of an enthusiastic audience. The CD insert lists it as being recorded at Paramount Studio M in Hollywood. I'm not sure what to make of that but maybe it was recorded at Paramount in front of invited guests. There were certainly plenty of them if that was the case and they make their presence felt.

The record kicks off with 'Five', an uptempo swinger in the bop, modal style that Jackie had developed and expanded over the years. His solo is a blazing one, well-shadowed by former students Hotep Idris Galeta on piano and Nat Reeves on bass. Carl Allen is the explosive drummer. In some ways this music reflects the fiery music Jackie played on Blue Note records in his prime, together with some of the more contemporary flourishes he had developed in recent times. 'Bird Lives' is, of course, a pulsating, driving homage to his early mentor and friend and he attacks it with vigour, the bop phrases spilling out furiously. Son Rene plays a similar, frenzied tenor solo and you realise how similar father and son sound. Not surprising of course as Rene was a pupil of his father's and as a child had asked for a saxophone, aged just nine. 'I didn't think he was going to be that interested in it,' McLean told Will Thornbury. At first, young Rene was given just a mouthpiece which he blew on 'day and night around the house for a full month. He was driving me crazy, he sounded so awful.' So Jackie gave him the neck of the instrument with the mouthpiece and he blew on that for another three weeks.

After that there was nothing for it but to give the boy a complete horn: 'He had a nice big tone. That's how I got him going.'

As 'Bird Lives' comes to a shuddering conclusion and the audience burst into spontaneous applause and calls, Jackie thanks them and adds: 'Bird Lives. No question about it, I feel him every day.' McLean's music had moved on, developed into his own very personal sound and style but he remembered his first major influence on alto sax every day of his life. That is how strong the bond between McLean and Parker was and how it remained. Even when he was deep into his more free jazz styles he would often contrast it by playing a club set or a record session with a batch of Parker staples like 'Confirmation', 'Scrapple from the Apple' and 'Barbados'. A year or so after recording this set he would take part in a Parker tribute disc.

Burt Bacharach's 'House Is Not a Home' is the ballad feature on *Dynasty* and McLean shows that he has further honed his skills as a balladeer. The lines are typically acerbic and cutting but somehow manage to convey a lot more bittersweet emotion than any sugary interpretation of this piece would offer. Jackie's horn conveys the full emotive force and pain of a broken romance and a house left bleak and empty by the departure of a partner.

'Third World Express' is an uptempo burner with the McLean alto hot and fiery through several choruses until Rene comes in on tenor and almost matches dad in blowing intensity and invention. Rene is also heard on soprano and flute on this session and the liner notes record that Jackie, in conversation with Will Thornbury, recalled the day in 1967 when his son came home with a flute. He could play it a little and kept practising but Jackie told him that although it was nice he should really concentrate on his horn (alto sax). Rene persisted and became so proficient on the flute that Jackie confessed to Thornbury that he became jealous when his son appeared to be 'moving out ahead of me'. So McLean senior bought a flute, practised hard and eventually caught up with his son. They played duets together but, eventually, 'he took off and I never did catch him again.' The track 'Dance Little Mandissa' on this CD gives a good example of Rene's exceptional talent as a flute soloist. He just about manages to eclipse his dad in solo intensity here although the alto solo is a scorcher too!

Tracks such as 'Zimbabwe' and 'Third World Express' emphasise the concentration on the African connection that Jackie was pursuing at this time. Many of his compositions were based on African rhythms and methods and he would frequently get the musicians in the band to play in traditional African costumes. 'King Tut's Strut' was composed by pianist Hotep Idris Galeta who was born in Cape Town, South Africa, and went to the United States in the early 1960s, later becoming a professor at the Hartt School. Hotep was highly rated by McLean who described him to a radio disc jockey as 'a gift from the creator to me'. He described Galeta's music as 'a mixture of Eastern music, African roots, a love of Horace Silver and a deep devotion'.

'J Mac's Dynasty', the title track, was written by Rene. Asked by Thornbury what it meant, Jackie replied, 'It just means that I'm creating a dynasty of young musicians that come under my influence and will go out and play, not just to fool around but to play great and continue with the business. In turn, they'll go out and do the same thing I have done.' Always the teacher, and officially so after he went to Hartford, Jackie looked ahead and trained not just good jazz musicians but future teachers and instructors like himself. Galeta is a good example but there are, of course, many, many others.

McLean was fifty-six years old when he recorded *Dynasty* with his son and several students but there was no diminution of the power, intensity and creativity of his alto sax lines. The disc features some of the most intense, inventive alto lines put on record up to that date and the leader is more than matched by the enthusiasm and full commitment of his sidemen. It is a powerful recorded testament.

If *Dynasty* represents jazz in the late 1980s, with its concentration on modal playing and free style excursions, McLean was still able to take a temporary step backwards and survey the earlier scene and his own roots, as he did at a concert recorded at the Théâtre de Boulogne-Billancourt in France on June 7th 1989. Along with other veterans like tenor man Johnny Griffin, baritone saxist Cecil Payne and a sterling rhythm section comprising Duke Jordan on piano, bassist Ron Carter and drummer Roy Haynes, Jackie played a tribute to Charlie Parker programme consisting of his own 'Bird Lives' and five Parker compositions.

There is no attempt here to play in a contemporary manner or to introduce recently acquired licks into this programme; this is a Parker tribute and bop is the style of play. Significantly perhaps, Jackie solos on all but one of these selections and we could almost be back in 1956 or, indeed, the 1940s. Jackie's solo on 'Parker's Mood' is deep blue, heartfelt and a wonderfully fresh variation on the bop blues style. Only once does he hint at new methods of expression developed over the years when he lets out a restrained *Let Freedom Ring*-style squeal but the rest of an extended and very inventive alto solo is pure bebop. Don Sickler follows him with a well-structured trumpet solo but it is the sheer intensity of that alto solo that lingers in the mind for long afterwards. Griffin plays complex, fractured lines; rather different from his usual straight-ahead manner and it may have been the force and content of McLean's solo segment that inspired him to try to excel himself here.

'Chasin' the Bird' also gets the full, head-on hard bop treatment with Cecil Payne starting off the solo sequence with crusty but flowing baritone lines. Jackie's solo is also full-on, bop inflexions flowing engagingly but with an attempt to produce something fresh and new within the confines of the classic bebop language. The same inventive intensity and joy of playing this music is evident on 'Big Foot' and 'Donna Lee' with everybody playing at an extremely high level of creativity. This was, after all, an ideal lineup for a tribute to Charlie Parker. McLean, Jordan and Haynes had all played with Bird: Jackie in clubs around NYC as a fellow-freelance, and the others as sidemen in his combos.

The CD, and there was a second volume to follow, was billed as *Birdology, A Tribute to Charlie Parker*, on the Birdology label (FDM 37014-2) and although it was a collective, specially assembled band, the unofficial leader and prime mover was Jackie McLean, Bird admirer extraordinary.

21

TIME WARP: TWO
PARKER'S MOOD

Jackie and Dollie are living in New York City's Lower East Side. It is a night when he has no engagement to play and they are relaxing at home. There is a loud knock at the door and Jackie finds Charlie Parker standing there, beaming at him and suggesting that they go out and find somewhere to play. It should be a quiet night in, peaceful, with a few drinks at home, maybe a game of chess and a relatively early night, but Parker is a larger than life character, difficult to resist when he wants friends to join him and Jackie is still in awe of him as the world's greatest modern alto player. The older man has got to know young Jackie, has heard him play on several occasions and seems to sense, almost to know, that he will be a star soloist in the future. For the present, though, all he wants is to encourage him and secure his company for the evening.

Jackie is hesitant still but Bird can be very persuasive; few up and coming jazz soloists can or would want to resist him and the very fact that he takes an interest in the younger musician is, in itself, quite a compliment. Jackie agrees to accompany Bird as long as he can bring Dollie along. The three of them leave the house and make for the area where most of the clubs are. Parker wants to find somewhere to play as he too is without an engagement but his restless spirit is looking for a base; somewhere to go in and blow.

They arrive at the Open Door and quickly try to set something up but this is a weeknight and the club has music at weekends only. Parker is persistent but the manager is having none of it. So they leave and walk further down into Greenwich Village and as they move along the sidewalk they gradually become aware that other musicians have joined them and are walking just a little way behind or to the side of the road. Jackie smiles as he recognises the faces of young acquaintances, a bass player, a trumpet man, a drummer, one or two that are not familiar and are, perhaps, still unknown generally and looking for a gig. What better way of finding a chance to play than attaching yourself to Parker and his friends? Wherever they end up is likely to be somewhere to blow, a place where music is available. They come to a place called Arthur's Tavern on Fourth Street and it looks a likely spot; a good few people are in and the bar is spacious and it looks as if the acoustic might be good. Parker settles on this place and takes Jackie with him to find the proprietor or manager. After being asked he says, 'Sure, go ahead,' and Parker beams one of his big, expansive smiles and they settle down in an alcove with drinks and Jackie hands the horn he has brought over to Bird. Parker rarely travels with his horn; in fact Parker rarely has a horn, mostly it is in a pawn shop or he's just sold it to raise money for a quick fix or whatever his current, pressing need happens to be. Or he's just plain lost it and has no ideas where he last left it.

Fortunately, on this night, all he wants to do is play, whether he gets paid or not; whether he has an audience or not, the requirement is to get up there and blow. He takes the horn, a rented alto as Jackie too is short on cash and not always too sure where the next gig is coming from; these two have, on occasions in the recent past, hired a horn that they both use, one gig after another. Parker runs his fingers over the keys and seems, after a minute or so, satisfied. He puts the saxophone to his lips and blows soundlessly as though testing it and then turns to Dollie who is watching him and smiles again, expansively. Then he puts his hand on Dollie's stomach and rubs it very, very gently; this is a superstition of Bird's, he does it to bring good luck before going up to play. A minute passes and Bird's smile flashes back on and he tells Dollie and Jackie that 'you have a little girl in there.' Dollie McLean is in fact pregnant at the time and many months later will give birth to the couple's daughter, Melonae, the original 'Little Melonae' from her father's records. Jackie smiles and shakes his head, Dollie smiles, neither of them taking it too seriously; they know Parker's eccentricities of old. Parker, satisfied, nods, gets up and walks onto the stage at the end of the room. Two other musicians are already up there and as Parker starts to play a blues they fall in hesitantly but willingly in support. Parker plays, as he always did, with full commitment and passion and soon gets the feet stomping and the heads nodding in the bar.

He finishes his solo and walks off the stage with no ceremony whatsoever and places the shared horn in the hand of his friend. Jackie gets up, smiles briefly at Bird and goes onto the stage and begins to play. The support from the other musicians is just as committed and brisk and the alto lines are very similar in style and phraseology to what has recently been played by Parker. Not quite though. At this time young Jackie is the eager student, Parker the master. Jackie is attempting to play lines with the same depth of feeling, the same passion and the same blues content as Bird's had, just as, in thirty years time, young alto sax players in their teens and twenties will hang on every note he plays and try to get something approximating his powerful sound and unique style into their playing. Jackie now is concentrating all his considerable skill and feeling into reproducing at least one aspect of the multi-functional Parker: his strong blues inflections. He too finishes his solo and returns to the table and his wife and friend.

Parker asks Jackie to come outside the club with him briefly, as he wants to talk about something private. Jackie smiles, shrugs at Dollie and then rises and follows Bird out of the doors.

Parker immediately starts to lecture him; it turns out he's been tipped off that young Jackie has been experimenting with hard drugs and the older man is keen to persuade him not to do it. He knows, only too well, the damage that heroin can do and is anxious to talk all young musicians into giving up or, better still, never starting. 'You know, Jackie,' Parker begins, 'man, you should try to be like Horace Silver and some of the younger musicians that's coming along today, and, and, and – get yourself together. You know man, you really ought to ... I feel responsible for, for what you're doing and you need to come on and kick me in the behind for this, you know?' Jackie shakes his head and looks embarrassed but Parker keeps on at him, keeps insisting. 'Kick me in the ass,' Parker says again and repeats it again and again until, reluctantly, Jackie takes aim and applies the required kick to Parker's posterior.

It is something that Jackie will remember, years afterwards, fondly recalling that his friend felt so badly about the poor example he was setting that he had to insist on this bizarre spectacle on the streets of Greenwich Village. And he will reflect, when he watches Clint Eastwood's film *Bird* and sees the incident re-enacted with Red Rodney as the kicker, that he was, in fact, the real young musician that Parker singled out. But then there always was a strong affinity between these two.[1]

22

RHYTHM OF THE EARTH

Charlie Parker was the father of modern jazz, the most influential alto soloist with players of just about every instrument coming under his spell. That is to take nothing from other innovative musicians who made such a contribution to bebop, people like Dizzy Gillespie, Bud Powell, Thelonious Monk and Kenny Clarke. All were important and, significantly, all of them played with Parker at one stage or other of the development of the music but Parker was the complete, virtuosic soloist and the writer of the bebop language.

Following him and playing in the new style came just about every alto player in jazz, with the only exceptions of note being the original Lee Konitz and the gifted Art Pepper, although the latter owed a lot to Parker in working out his own unique approach.

From all of the musicians who followed Parker and were active in his lifetime only a very few emerge as significant players to continue and expand the tradition. A soloist like Sonny Stitt, for example, played in the Parker style for all of his life without ever changing at all. He always claimed to have developed that style of playing independently of Parker but that is a statement that I feel we must view with suspicion. It is much more likely that he was influenced strongly by Parker in the beginning without being aware of it and maybe, even, hearing Parker phrases from other musicians who had picked them up on the road. Julian 'Cannonball' Adderley was very close to the Parker sound and style during his most productive years, so much so that baritone player Gerry Mulligan, in a blindfold test in a magazine, thought that a live performance by the Adderley quintet was by Parker; although he awarded it a thousand stars for 'Bird' he said that he wouldn't buy the record. Adderley never changed his style or approach and died relatively young but he was a good example of the best of the Parker alto followers. Phil Woods was very close to Parker in the early days and after Bird's death married his bereaved partner, Chan. But his own personal style evolved into an alto language of his own; it did not change over the years and remains the same at the time of writing.

Only two major alto saxophonists have emerged over the longer term who have extended Parker's style: Jackie McLean and Ornette Coleman. Coleman's contribution is of major significance but it was to create a different and simpler approach to contemporary jazz playing and composing and is, of course, the subject for a separate book and beyond the scope of this one. McLean is the one important alto soloist who, having been seen and heard to play in the bop style developed by Parker and his associates, developed and refined his own sound and style, and extended and added to the language of bop and free jazz.

Jackie himself commented: 'I have never been in the forefront of any new style, but I have been able to align myself with different styles and maybe add to them.'[1] A modest enough claim indeed for somebody who embraced bop, hard bop and free music and added his own unique sound and compositional skills to each. In the long term, however, I believe McLean will be seen as the logical successor to Charlie Parker, the musician who extended certain aspects of Parker's style, incorporated it into his own and took the music gradually forward at his own pace. He certainly represents the most advanced hard bop playing throughout the early and later 1960s and was one of the most inventive and forward-looking musicians in the period between 1964 and 1996. Significantly, when he was at the peak of his playing powers, around 1960–61, he did not condemn the work of the new wave of players that were coming up at the time, as many other established soloists did, but chose instead to find inspiration and new paths to follow. He acknowledged publicly the inspiration he had received from listening to Ornette Coleman and John Coltrane and was probably listening closely to Eric Dolphy and, very briefly, Albert Ayler. His position was always that, if the music was moving in new directions and finding fresh methods of expression, he could find inspiration in those new sounds, incorporate them into his own work and build upon the new music he produced. Examples like *Let Freedom Ring* and *One Step Beyond* are the best illustrations of his development of new ideas and new music. And, because he was deservedly well-regarded as a bopper before he started to play more free jazz, the jazz public and critics respected his new music and this, in turn, gave a much needed boost to musicians like Grachan Moncur, Bobby Hutcherson, Walter Davis Jr., Herbie Lewis and Tony Williams.

Where does McLean stand in terms of overall achievement and commitment to the music? I believe that, in the last analysis, his contribution will be seen as having consolidated, expanded and added to the legacy of Charlie Parker. Although he made important contributions to the development of new jazz, played his own take on free style and helped hundreds if not thousands of young musicians to find their way and, in some cases, receive recognition they might never have had without him, his own very finest work on record will be found on his late Prestige and early Blue Note recordings. Here, his extension of the Parker solo style and a deep blue, bittersweet, often acrid tone moved the music forward in the best way it could move forward, through honing, refining and finding a redefinition of the bop style as laid down by Parker and his closest associates.

In other words, McLean was a good, strong, inventive free jazz alto player but he was also a brilliant, wonderfully creative soloist in the hard bop manner and in his own interpretation of it. Check out on records how many times Jackie played a free jazz date only to follow it up a short time later with a more traditional recording. Check out the fact that even when he was deep into playing in the new style he was playing safe with recordings like *Tippin' the Scales* in 1962 or *The Jackie McLean Quintet* date of the same year. Listen to the *Birdology* tribute to Charlie Parker (FDM 37014-2) from 1989 where he tears it up with relish on six Parker compositions with other veterans of bebop like Roy Haynes and Duke Jordan. And if any other proof were needed that McLean was, and remained, first and foremost a bopper, listen again to his version of 'Bird Lives' on *Dynasty* (Triloka 181-2) and his words at the conclusion of this piece: 'Bird lives, no question about it, I feel him every day.'

* * *

As if to contradict the above, on March 12th and 13th 1992 Jackie recorded *Rhythm of the Earth* for the Birdology label. It was a return to the Van Gelder studio at Englewood Cliffs and the man McLean described as the best sound engineer he ever worked with. The music is free flowing, modal in style and further away from the hard bop sound than Jackie usually reached after the 1980s. The music was inspired, according to the altoist's brief sleevenotes, as a tribute to the Dogon people and their contributions to the rhythm of the earth. The Sirius System, a group of stars, was said to have been known to the Dogon people for over 300 years, but not to the western world until a powerful telescope was built in 1950 and the stars were visible. How the Dogon people were able to know about these stars without the aid of modern technology remains a mystery. The Dogon people live in Mali in Africa and reference to them and their ancient knowledge of star clusters may have been because McLean, at this time, was studying African cultures in his quest to learn everything about African-American music through the ages. It was, after all, part of the complete picture on the music and its origins that he was trying to teach at the university and the Artists Collective.

Along with his students, Steve Davis, trombone, Alan Jay Palmer on piano and Eric McPherson at the drums, the band included guest musicians Roy Hargrove and vibes man Steve Nelson. Unlike many records McLean made in later years, this session is firmly in the contemporary modal style and, as usual, it features his students generously in solo and ensemble playing. The title track 'Rhythm of the Earth' kicks off with a drum burst from McPherson followed by a fairly dense ensemble by the horns which slowly segues into a McLean alto solo: intense, acrid, modal and building slowly but effectively over several choruses. Nelson's vibes are prominent in a supporting role and the rhythm section pushes purposefully. This track also has changes of tempo with the altoist moving suddenly from medium upwards as he builds his solo. This is very much the new McLean, the committed experimenter and boundary pusher. Roy Hargrove, very much the up-coming and impressive new trumpet voice in 1992, has a good solo here following on from the leader and offering his own take on modal styling and changing tempi. The piece moves comfortably from medium to fast to slow and back to medium and there is a neat, probing vibes solo. Trombonist Steve Davis, one of Jackie's most successful and interesting students at that time, is one of the last to solo, his lines showing invention and, in the slow passages, economy.

This is McLean doing what he did best, playing in the contemporary manner of the day and adding his own unique sound and method of improvising to the music. This selection lasts for fifteen minutes but unlike many long jazz tracks it does not seem long; there is always plenty to attract the listener and lots of variety in the arrangement and execution.

'For Hofsa' is a slow, somewhat mournful ballad, written by McLean and played by him in solo with a strong, blues-based melancholy that is far more like his regular sound and style through the decades. Hargrove sounds right at home on this one too and his solo is delivered with something of a swagger. 'Sirius

System' was written by pianist Alan Jay Palmer and sounds like a complex hard bop line with contemporary additions. Hargrove is flying from the start and Jackie follows with a churning, hard-edged solo as bass and drums thrash around him. In many ways this CD, made towards the end of the most active period of Jackie's recording career, indicates the best of his playing, rooted strongly in the past and the hard bop era but taking on board modal and other more contemporary methods of expression. You can sense, almost hear, the two-way interaction being formulated as master and pupils inspire each other and produce good, solid, inventive jazz in the process.

More and more, except for occasional link-ups with other veterans for specific projects like the *Parker Tribute* CDs, Jackie was playing live and recording with his current or ex-students and often a mixture of both. The music received a boost from the enthusiasm and occasionally the mistakes that were turned to advantage by the experienced McLean. He himself became freshly inspired by his young charges. As always, his music was fresh on the day it was played or recorded, never pinned down permanently to one style or manner of playing. Open to new challenges and new directions, no matter who or what caused the change, McLean's music continued through the 1980s and 1990s to find fresh avenues of expression, as it always had from the very beginning.

23

WORKING MUSICIAN

If the whole of the 1970s had been bleak and barren with little work for jazz musicians, even the very best, the 1980s saw an upturn in interest in the music generally and more gigs for Jackie McLean in particular. He spent much time on the road with his group, playing regularly in the United States, Europe and, particularly Japan, where he was so popular that they opened jazz cafes named after him.

1988 was an especially busy year with engagements at the Mount Fuji Jazz Festival in Japan and regular playing in the USA including a gig at the Catalina Bar and Grill in Los Angeles in June, reported in the *Los Angeles Times*. As he told journalist Zan Stewart, with reference to his functions with the Artists Collective, the university programme and his live playing, 'that makes three big things on my resume of life.' Then he added 'Bird, Pres, Hawk, they died great saxophone players. When I die I want people to remember my other accomplishments.' Stewart mentioned that in addition to other duties, Jackie taught 'little kids, three to four years old.' He taught them fundamentals of music such as how to count. Jackie told his interviewer that there was a lot of work to do if the youngsters were to have a better life. He said that he didn't know 'why I'm pushed to this thing' but I suspect that he had a good idea. Asked what advice he would give to youngsters wanting to make a career in straight-ahead jazz, he said, 'I prepare my kids for a hard life.' A lot of jobs were being taken by electronic performers but there would always be an audience for acoustic jazz. 'This is a beautiful music full of feeling and sound that is too important to die.'

At this time a trip to California was unusual for Jackie who was working mostly in Europe and Japan. His U.S. gigs were mainly confined to the east coast and, specifically, New York City. But, like all good soloists trying to make a living, he took whatever was available, no matter where. I suspect he would have gone to Outer Mongolia quite happily if a gig had been offered. He told Zan Stewart that he was working with his own quartet of young musicians and also, occasionally, with all-star groups including Cedar Walton, Donald Byrd and other old friends but this was mainly for high profile and presumably reasonably well paid gigs such as the Mount Fuji festival in Japan. He also said, true to form, that he preferred working with his regular group because instead of playing standards 'we're playing fresh stuff written by the young guys in the band and myself.' But he conceded that he threw in things that people wanted to hear such as McLean originals like 'Little Melonae' and 'Minor March'.

He confirmed that he was still open-minded about the sort of music played. 'I play everything,' he said, claiming to go out, away from the melodic side and 'holler and scream on my horn'. He said he liked also to get funky and play the blues, get involved in some chord changes and play some intricate things. It did not have to be one set style.

In fact, nobody in jazz offered as much variety in his music at this time and he continued to do so throughout his career and up to the very end of his life. For McLean, no music from his past was too old hat or unworthy of being played today and no music was so far out that he would not attempt to play in that style himself. Had anybody asked him to name his favourite style of jazz, as far as personal choice for playing was concerned, I suspect he would have said 'all of them'.

By the end of the 1980s, he had, it seems, slowed down, at least sufficiently to hand over some of his more arduous teaching and lecturing roles and had even found time for occasional practising. 'I keep my chops up and I'm playing better than ever', he said to Zan Stewart in 1988. Although Jackie was only fifty-six at this time, the many years on the road, the scuffling in NYC in the 1950s, the drug busts and the hard teaching schedule would all have taken their toll. Wisely, he began to find a way of carrying on doing what he enjoyed most, playing and teaching but on a reduced scale that left some time for practice and, even more important to him, being at home. He handed over responsibility for some of his teaching duties to others and if he began taking less gigs than he could have comfortably accommodated it was probably because he still felt that he was being offered much less money than he was entitled to. And yet, although he was most adamant that he would not accept gigs for 'silly money', another statement made in the 1980s really put his true attitude into perspective. Talking about enjoying seeing an audience hear him play he said: 'If the people enjoy it and I leave the stage feeling good about it, that's the greatest reward, man. There's no money can make up for that.'

Music was always in Jackie's head, he said on many occasions, and he claimed that he often dreamed about it. He had loved music since he was a child and had been brought up listening to Billie Holiday, Louis Armstrong and Duke Ellington. His mother played spirituals and gospel records and young Jackie would burst into tears, moved by the music. There could have been little doubt in the McLean household in Harlem about what he would be when he left school.

Oddly enough, although Jackie had one of the most distinctive alto sounds in jazz with a bitter, often slightly sharp but passionate tone, he never planned to play alto and possibly only settled on it when he heard Parker for the first time. 'It's like an alto but it's really a tenor coming from the inside of me,' he said in the interview with Stewart. 'I've never really liked the sound of the alto except for Bird and Sonny Stitt.' If he hadn't heard Bird, he said, he would probably have switched to tenor and he claimed to have been in love with Dexter Gordon, Ben Webster, Lester Young and the others; trying to make the alto sound like Dexter or Lester was how he came to get his unique alto sound. He didn't specify who the others were that he admired but it will not take a lot of working out for jazz enthusiasts.

* * *

It was around this time that he admitted that in the past he had been somewhat bitter about the fact that although recognition and appreciation of his efforts were plentiful, material reward had evaded him. As was often the case, however, he managed to turn that into something more positive. As he said in 1988: 'I'm comfortable right now. I don't seem to be in quest of material things and there's nothing I can do about the past.' He was, he claimed, just seeking health and happiness, to live in peace, have children and live in a healthy world.

It would seem that the past hung heavily for McLean. Nobody who uses hard drugs escapes the ravages and scars that they leave and the way they make home life difficult, if not impossible. There were many approaches to the way addicts dealt with their problem at this time and although many, the majority in fact, ended up so enslaved and dependent on their habit that they resorted to stealing and gross anti-social behaviour to feed it, others, few in number but significant, managed to keep it under control for the most part and restrict intake of the drug to the minimum. Jackie was most likely one of the latter as he always managed to maintain a steady home life and had the support of his wife through all the bad as well as the good years. Looking back, once he had shaken off the dreadful addiction and had himself become a counsellor helping others to quit the habit, he must have felt tremendous relief, considerable gratitude to Dollie and a lot of remorse for the wasted years when he was not functioning at full pressure.

It all went back to the legacy of Charlie Parker: on the one hand the enabling inspiration, the standard of improvising and playing alto that set many young players on their way and, on the other, the totally negative drug addiction which, because he succombed to it, many young musicians copied.

McLean's addiction had led to a seven-year-layoff from playing alto in clubs but in 1975 he had secured a gig at the Five Spot on St. Mark's Place in NYC. According to Gary Giddins, writing much later in *Jazz Times*,[2] the club was packed every night with musicians and fans. Giddins reported that he played 'a barbed and biting solo', disappeared from the stage and came back a little later and played 'an even more rambunctious second solo, topped off with a mocking "Frère Jacques" quote.' The purpose of the second solo, more intense and passionate than the first, had been to reach Sonny Rollins, who had been in the audience, at the back of the club, 'I didn't want Sonny to think I hadn't done my homework.' The other feature, for which he showed Giddins the evidence after the set concluded, was that he had played all through with a reed that had an eighth of an inch gash in it; absolutely unplayable to most people. It was a highly successful gig and if the newly refurbished Five Spot did not last very long, Jackie did; he was back as a soloist eady to meet his public again and the next two decades would see him re-establish himself as one of the major alto sax stylists in jazz.

* * *

In the 1980s Jackie was fortunate to have a regular group consisting of his son Rene on saxes and flute, Raymond Williams on trumpet, trombonist Steve Davis and two old stagers in pianist Alan Jay Palmer and drummer Eric McPherson. The bassist was Phil Bowler, another young musician who had studied with Jackie for some years. This unit shook down and played fairly regularly if intermittently when McLean was exceptionally busy at the university or the Collective, which often happened. He continued to delegate more and more work at those seats of learning, thus freeing himself up for live gigs and time with the family.

This band worked more in the nineties than the eighties but it continued McLean's lifelong policy of picking and playing with bright young musicians for the majority of his gigs. This is not to suggest that he wasn't thoroughly exhilarated and happy linking up with the likes of Cedar Walton and Billy Higgins when the opportunities presented themselves. Chances to play with his old mates came mainly when they were booked to play concerts for the Artists Collective and Jackie was the man who booked them.

Alex Henderson argued in a review that the music played by Jackie McLean on his CD *Fire and Love* recorded in 1997 was not unlike the Blue Note recordings of the 1960s.[2] He described it as 'aggressive post-bop' and 'invigorating hard bop/post-bop', and I must concede that he has a point. It also adds to my suspicions, voiced earlier in this narrative, that McLean's overall favourite jazz style, in spite of all his development and championing of avant-garde free music, was Charlie Parker-inspired bebop and its derivative, hard bop. As Sonny Rollins noted, he and McLean always represented the hard bop element from the earliest days and their individual contributions were well received at that time by people who were alienated by Miles Davis' 'cool approach'. That started back in the early 1950s when both Rollins and McLean were in Miles' band but both of them retained elements of that style of playing throughout the next four decades. Jackie recalled as late as 2001 in a radio interview, answering a question about how Parker had affected his life, that Bird had suggested the next step for him in music. After hearing him for the first time, Jackie knew how to proceed, how to develop as a soloist and he felt sure that this realisation applied to others like Sonny Rollins and John Coltrane.

McLean was adept at springing surprises or, put another way, not always doing what was expected of him. At a live session in

Peruggia, Italy, in 1983, he played in a reunion band that included Bobby Hutcherson on vibes, old favourite drummer Billy Higgins and bassist Herbie Lewis. The music is, true to form, a mixture of bop and free and as intense and passionate as always.

The 1980s represented a culmination of all that he had learned through some thirty-odd years as a professional musician. His life at the university must also have been very satisfying: working his way up from having a temporary teaching post in 1970, through establishing it as a regular post, becoming assistant professor and then full professor, and finishing with a full degree course in African-American music and studies. It also enabled him to enjoy working in the classroom and to stay at home when he wished, only picking the riper or more remunerative live gigs when he felt like playing.

Considering how few opportunities he had found for both playing and recording in the 1970s, the eighties marked the return to live action and a variety of playing opportunities which, fortunately, would continue into the next decade.

24

THE SOUND OF JAZZ

The sound of jazz is represented by each individual soloist on his or her instrument. It is an expression of individuality and personality. Where it is desirable, if not obligatory, for classical trumpeters, for example, to obtain a certain pure, unwavering sound which makes them all sound alike, a jazz musician looks for and hopes eventually to find a personal, unique sound on each instrument. Few people could ever confuse Lester Young with Coleman Hawkins, Sonny Rollins, John Coltrane or Hank Mobley. The reason is, of course, that they all sound different, unique, although they all played the contemporary jazz of their day on the same instrument: tenor saxophone. Equally, it would be hard to fail to recognise Benny Carter, Johnny Hodges, Willie Smith or Lee Konitz because although they all played alto sax they came from different schools of jazz and each had a personal sound.

When Charlie Parker came on the scene around the late 1930s, he came in with, seemingly, a whole new alto sound and a whole new school of jazz: bebop. From that time onwards, with very, very few exceptions, every alto player wanted to sound like Parker and most jazz musicians wanted to play the new bebop. Jackie McLean was unique in that he developed his own special and distinctive sound on alto sax right from the very beginning. Even though in the early days he was trying to play exactly like Parker; it was that stridency in his tone that set him apart even from his very first recordings; that is from the late 1940s until Mingus climbed on his back and refused to move in 1957. In the mid-fifties, Jackie's lines were almost pure Parker but the sound he delivered them with was uniquely McLean. Unlike Cannonball Adderley and Phil Woods, to name just two of hundreds, he had his own sound from the word go whereas the others sounded and played just like Bird in the early years. As American writer and author Gary Giddins put it 'McLean's primary home is his pitch, a curiously individual way of bending the tempered scale so that his every note is an expression of personality and vision.'[1] It is a good description. Add to it Ira Gitler's 'Jackie's horn can cut a hole in your heart and let the night pour through'[2] and you have an idea of what McLean sounds like before you hear him.

Although not an innovator in the strictest sense, McLean was unique in that he continued and expanded the jazz language of Charlie Parker and began to expand the free jazz scene in the mid-sixties and take his own solo and group playing in new and ever more challenging directions. The force of his personality is well documented by the number of alto saxophonists who, like Abraham Burton, sound very much like him on the instrument. Jackie's sound changed subtly over the years as will be indicated by listening to an early Prestige recording, then a Blue Note from around 1959–60, a disc like *Let Freedom Ring* in 1963, and finally his late sound of the 1980s and '90s as represented by discs like *Dynasty* on Triloka and *Rhythm of the Earth* on Birdology.

It is not a case of major change at any point but rather just an inventive variation of pitch and intensity to suit the music of the moment, in the same way that Sonny Rollins changed his sound on almost every record he made between 1957 and 1963. This mark of the constantly exploring, constantly experimenting, constantly inventive jazz soloist. At the other extreme to this would be somebody like Sonny Stitt or Johnny Hodges who, although brilliant and inventive soloists, never changed from what they learned to play and the way they learned to play it in the very beginning to the day they died.

Perhaps because he was a multi-faceted player who embraced bop, hard bop and the free jazz movement in the 1960s, Jackie was, on balance, an underrated soloist for much of his life. Like his friend and frequent Blue Note band-mate Hank Mobley, McLean always put in a hard-working performance on everything he recorded, whether he was the leader or not. Although he was nowhere near as neglected as Mobley and far more successful overall, there were many occasions when critics and would-be jazz experts failed to understand what he was doing and consequently denied him the support and encouragement he deserved. There were many instances of critics in magazines and newspapers supplying damning critiques of his recordings, sometimes tempered with faint praise.

A good example of Jackie changing pace, briefly, and doing something a little challenging and different, was his October 1959 Blue Note recording of *Swing, Swang, Swingin'*. In this session, Jackie worked his own particular hard bop-based but lyrical magic on five hardy and popular standards, one blues and one jazz standard in the making, Benny Golson's 'Stable Mates'. The bop stylings are there of course, the modern jazz phrasing and the solid, driving beat but the music is essentially bright, melodic, lyrical and McLean's individual way of playing is beginning to emerge, his sound coming over as very much his own even if there are just a few Parker phrases remaining. In the May 26th 1960 edition of *Down Beat* magazine, reviewer Barbara J. Gardner gave the LP three and a half stars, slightly better than good in *DB*'s rating system and slightly less than very good. The review overall is quite enthusiastic as she talks about Jackie's 'beauty of expression' and calls him a 'fundamental swinger'. But consider the opening and closing paragraphs of her review. She says she detests having to give a trite opinion and that if she should read one more review suggesting that McLean is a faint echo of Bird, straight to Nutville she would go. 'Yet here it is,' she continues, 'and this album leaves no honest alternative to that view.' No mention is made of McLean making a change of pace and playing mainly medium tempos or slow ballads throughout; no suggestion that this is precisely the sort of record that might well appeal to people frightened off by the more aggressive, uptempo forays of the hard bop of the day. At the end she assures readers that there is 'no "future promise" here' and that there is no indication that McLean is searching for identity. 'Apparently he has found his groove and intends to work within its confines.'

How wrong can you be? It is easy to be wise with hindsight and perhaps I am being unkind in singling out this review when there were many very similar but I do maintain that there were more than a few signs of McLean finding his own voice and also signs that he was looking ever eagerly towards finding new methods of expression. His sound was changing fairly frequently from 1955 to 1960, the year this set was released, a sure sign of a search for identity and growth. There is also a reference in this disc's liner notes by Ira Gitler to an article by British writer Michael James which reveals the ways in which McLean differs from Parker. Had Gardner read the very good liner notes she might surely have thought twice about her 'faint echo of Bird' condemnation. Insight and a thorough knowledge of jazz are contained in James' quoted words on those liner notes: 'There seems to be every reason to believe that although he has already made several good records his potential is by no means completely fulfilled .... [He] is still very much a man to watch.'

Some critics were still not watching but by the 1990s almost all had come to appreciate an original stylist with deep roots in the tradition. The *Swing, Swang, Swingin'*, album was not the only time that Jackie decided on change to a slower pace from his current work and a change of personnel. A second album of ballads recorded in 1998 was called *Nature Boy,* and as with the earlier disc, he did not call it a 'ballads' set as John Coltrane had done with one of his albums in 1961 only to receive a stream of very harsh criticism for playing in a simple style and sticking closely to the melodies. In fact neither of McLean's discs sound particularly like ballad albums and the first has some uptempo selections and can and does sound like a typical hard bop session at times. The *Nature Boy* album, first issued in Japan on the Somethin' Else label (TOCJ 68045) has more intimate ballads, those that cry out for slow or medium treatment and a touch of gentle lyricism. Jackie also abandoned temporarily his policy of employing mainly young players, recruited from members of his current band or recent students. There were times, and this was one of them, when he felt the need to play in the company of a high profile, hard swinging professional rhythm section and he duly recruited pianist Cedar Walton, bassist David Williams and Billy Higgins at the drums.

No contest this time: the reviews were, in the great majority, favourable and Jackie's change of pace certainly paid off. Musicians generally agree that it is more difficult to play straight ballads and get them right than play hard swinging bop where, although the soloist is improvising and fashioning fresh variations all the time, he can recover swiftly from a mistake or a doubtful choice of note or two. Playing a ballad with warmth and feeling and sticking closely to the melody leaves him no place to hide.

Listen to the opening track of *Nature Boy*, and it is immediately apparent that you are hearing a master soloist who has a very special way with a ballad. 'You Don't Know What Love Is' is played with warm, sincere feeling and a measure of melancholy always apparent in Jackie's best work. The alto lines are obviously offering a complete change of pace: lyrical melodies played straight in bebop mode, and even the extreme hardness of tone that was McLean's trademark almost all through his career is missing. It is as though Jackie is saying, 'Yes, I can play hard and straight bebop and free style jazz but there are times when I can just play a programme of great standards with warmth and passion.' All the mystery and other worldliness of that strange ballad 'Nature Boy' can be heard in Jackie's reading where he states the melody slowly before upping the tempo and swinging it with the rhythm section cruising along with him. There is a gem of a piano solo here from Walton to add to the delights on this album.

If I have emphasised Jackie's predilection for employing young musicians on tour and in the studios it is because that is mainly what he did. But there were were times when only a seasoned rhythm section of the absolute top rank would do and this was one. Walton's accompaniment is just what any good soloist desires, sensitive, intuitive and constantly supportive. The same holds true for the crisp, inventive drumming of Higgins, and Williams plays bass with a big, ripe sound and just the right choice of notes for each phrase. Together they generate swing, easily and naturally, an intransigent, almost impossible to define quality that you only recognise and understand when you hear it.

'I Can't Get Started' is the sort of standard that has been played by jazz soloists incessantly since trumpeter Bunny Berigan laid down an impeccable recorded version back in 1937. Even so, Jackie's version on *Nature Boy* is fresh and unique if only in the way he phrases the melody and gently, caressingly embellishes it with that bitter sweet alto sound of his.

They say that less is more on occasions and this is one McLean disc where he plays less notes than usual but achieves more in feeling and intensity on a set of familiar standards. 'What Is This Thing Called Love' swings along gracefully with the rhythm section lightly propelling him along almost invisibly; they are not in any way prominent but their presence is felt rather than heard. Walton's solo is, once again, a gem, flowing briskly, quoting from old bop licks, driving into the return of the alto soloist and then it is left to Jackie and a typical Billy Higgins solo to wrap things up in style.

Perhaps the ultimate ballad performance here is Jackie's solo on 'I Fall in Love Too Easily'. It is, again, a pretty straight reading, never straying far from the melody but played with such cool assurance and power that it is difficult, hearing this version, to accept that you have heard the song hundreds of times in the past. The album is rounded off with fine renditions of 'Star Eyes', now almost an alto soloist's bop anthem, 'Smoke Gets in Your Eyes', a real, seldom heard oldie, and the unlikely but effective 'A Nightingale Sang in Berkeley Square'.

On every one of these ballads Jackie is in his element, playing with relaxed skill and obvious enjoyment, quite possibly representing the least adventurous of anything he recorded over the last forty years but producing a delightful CD that should be in every jazz enthusiast's collection. No disrespect to the young players Jackie worked with most of the time but this wasn't just the best rhythm section he could find, it was the only one suitable for this job. Together this quartet produced an unlikely but definitely essential Jackie McLean record. And considering how late in his career it was made, it does rather make a nonsense of the theory that jazz musicians are well past their best in later life and unable to produce major works. It lacks the intensity and invention of discs like *Jackie's Bag* and *Let Freedom Ring* and half a dozen others but it is still an excellent jazz session by any standards.

25

TIME WARP: THREE
FAREWELL: ONE

Jackie has been playing in a bar in NYC and he has consumed a large amount of alcohol. Sometimes drinking a lot during the course of a gig or, more often, after it occurs, that's the way it goes. He is getting into a cab to go home, feeling slightly the worse for wear and Charlie Parker is there, ostensibly to help him. Bird takes his horn or, strictly speaking, takes the shared horn that he and Jackie have rented and have been using between them for a week or so. 'Here let me take this,' Parker says as Jackie struggles to get himself settled in the back of the cab. Somebody, one of the party of four or five people that have attached themselves to Bird and Jackie, tells the cab driver to take off and the vehicle moves away from the kerbside as Jackie realises that he no longer has possession of the saxophone that he and Bird rented on 48th Street. This could be bad news, Jackie reflects as he drives home, tired and feeling the effects of a night of music, audience reaction and, rather too much drink. It is true that they both rented it and are both responsible but Jackie knows, from bitter past experience, that horns in Parker's possession, whether he owns them or not, tend to go missing frequently or end up in the pawn shop. Still it is late, it has been a good night for music and he is tired; time to worry about his horn later.

Two days later, McLean and Parker cross paths in town and, sure enough, Bird no longer has the saxophone. It is in the pawnshop and it will cost a good sum of money to get it back.

Jackie is not best pleased and he says so. Having a close relationship with the older musician, the man who has represented so much to him in terms of influence, help and encouragement, makes it difficult to be angry with him for long. Besides it is not in Jackie's nature. But the number of times this or something similar has happened, aggravates the normally placid and calm Jackie and he walks away feeling irritated with Parker.

On Sunday Jackie has a gig at the Open Door club in the evening and he is back there playing up a storm. Charlie Parker arrives late in the evening in a party with Nica De Koenigswarter, the lady they call the jazz baroness; a woman from one of the aristocratic families in Britain who loves jazz and has been a patroness to the likes of Parker, Thelonious Monk and many others. Parker is enthusiastic about McLean's playing which he has persuaded the others in his party to come and hear and he praises Jackie warmly even if the younger man seems a little cool and aloof towards him. It is too late now and maybe he should forget it but he is still thinking about that horn that he lost in a moment of carelessness.

The gig is over and Parker offers to drop McLean off at his home in the car the party arrived in. 'No, that's all right, I'll get a cab,' Jackie says because he is still a little angry with him and this time he wants his friend to know it. A few days later Jackie is in town and he buys a newspaper before boarding a passing bus. He sits on the bus looking out of the window at the activity in New York and goes several blocks before even glancing at the *New York Post* sitting on his lap. It is a mighty shock when he does start reading it and sees that Charlie Parker is dead; he has died in the apartment of the baroness, where he had gone after feeling ill a few days earlier. McLean gets off the bus in tears and heads for the musicians' union offices on foot. For a time he is in a state of shock and disbelief. And when he arrives at the union office he is told that Parker's body is still in the mortuary and they are waiting for somebody to go there and identify it.

Still in a state of shock and confusion, Jackie heads downtown to Birdland, the jazz club named after Parker. A very distressed McLean remonstrates with the owner there, telling him that Bird is dead, Bird is registered as an unknown male at the mortuary and he had better go and – 'go down there and identify Bird's body, man.' There is some more talk, some angry exchanges and an altercation develops which has been fanned by the flames of McLean's shock, anger and sense of guilt and frustration. He is told at the club to mind his own business and to get out of there. Jackie says, 'Well, you named this club Birdland, you named it after him, why don't you go down there?' But he is told that he doesn't work there anymore and he must get out. So he leaves, still frustrated, still hurt and angry and it will be more than a year before he will work at Birdland again.

Jackie finds it difficult to forgive himself for the way he spoke to Parker on that last Sunday at the Open Door. Being blacklisted at Birdland means nothing to him, he will pick up gigs at plenty of other venues for this is 1955 and jazz is thriving, bop is still relatively new and fresh; a cool new jazz for a whole new generation of young enthusiasts. But parting from Parker with a curt refusal of his offer of a lift, even if it wasn't Bird's car, and losing his friend three or four days later: that is a deep pain that will not heal for a long time. Maybe never, fully. 'Oh man. It was awful,' he says. 'I missed the moment when I could have had one more moment with him, if I hadn't been over acting, you know?'

Jackie does not go to the funeral. He can't face it. 'I couldn't, I just couldn't go, you know? I couldn't be, couldn't be a part of that, you know? And it was terrible, especially for me, you know?'

Parker's death heralded the beginning, in many ways, of the mature, the new, fully professional, Jackie McLean. It was the year he made his first LP as leader and joined a top group as saxophonist in George Wallington's quintet. He would record with

Wallington at the Café Bohemia, play gigs there and soon secure his own recording contract with Prestige Records.

Now he is on his own. He has his family and his friends but his main inspiration for becoming a jazz musician is gone. Over the next four years he will compensate for his loss to some extent by visiting and helping the second great inspiration of his life, Lester Young, the man who originally inspired Parker to seek and find a fresh new language of jazz. Lester has not managed to come to terms with life in the bitter struggle and cold climate of trying to make a living playing a tenor saxophone. He is only content and fulfilled on the rare occasions when he goes out on a gig, rounds up a rhythm section and plays into the small hours. For the rest he either stays in his room or goes to the cinema where he will often stay and watch a movie through two or three times before returning to his bleak hotel room. He does not have long to live and he does not have many visitors. One regular though is Jackie McLean, the next important voice on jazz alto, bringing him cigarettes and gin, on and off, until Young dies in 1959 at the early age of forty-nine.

Parker and Young. Two great jazz soloists, pace setters for the jazz community, great when they play but unable to handle the ups and downs, the highs and fearsome lows, the trivialities and tragedies of the jazz life. Jackie McLean is on the threshold of a great career as a soloist but he will need every ounce of his strength, resolve and ambition not to fall into the same traps as his friends did, and to carve out a career and life with his wife and family that is completely fulfilling.

Fortunately time is on his side.[1]

26

FAREWELL: TWO

WWUH radio station in Hartford, Connecticut, broadcasts 'Public Alternative Radio' which certainly includes plenty of jazz. Former WWUH Programme Director Sue Terry was the first recipient of a degree from the Hartt School's jazz programme in 1982. Terry is a reed player, well known in NYC jazz circles and she has played frequently in the city. Quoted on the radio station website, she recalled McLean's kindness and encouragement when she was a student and his expansive knowledge of jazz history. She talked about Jackie and his wife Dollie ensuring that students at the collective and concertgoers were exposed 'to musical styles usually neglected by American pop culture'.

She recalled a gig in 1982, sponsored by the Artists Collective, when McLean was reunited with his old sparring partner Donald Byrd on trumpet, Don DePalma on piano, Nat Reeves, who was then a teacher at Hartt, on bass, and Mike DuQuette on drums. She could not recall a single individual tune played that night but she had a vivid memory of McLean 'leaning into the microphone, eyes closed, his face contorted as he silenced an otherwise noisy crowd with his horn's raging beauty.' Nearly two decades later, Terry interviewed McLean live in the WWUH studios on June 19th 2001.[1]

She recalled that 2001 had been very eventful for McLean (were there any years that were not?) and their interview was a few days before he played one of his last concerts at the Artists Collective with the Cedar Walton Trio. In November 2000 the

University of Hartford had officially changed its jazz department's name to 'The Jackie McLean Institute of Jazz'. And to top that the National Endowment for the Arts had bestowed their annual Jazz Master award on him in January 2001. In spite of all this, according to Terry, 'Jackie remained humble and gracious, preferring to speak about the accomplishments of some of the young musicians whose lives he'd touched through his teaching.'

One of those young musicians had vivid memories of visiting the Hartt School on the University of Hartford campus in the autumn of 1984. Trombonist Steve Davis recalled that the autumn leaves were falling and the reds and golds provided a beauty of landscape all around. His next memory of Hartt was from winter 1985 when he was auditioned by Jackie McLean. After a cordial greeting the young trombonist played an unaccompanied version of Gershwin's 'Summertime'. Jackie expressed some enthusiasm according to Davis, writing on the Hartt School website.[2] Then McLean sat down at the piano and began to play some 'exotic, hip chords'. He said, 'OK son. Let's see what you can do with these.'

What Davis could do with those was enough for McLean to encourage the young man to take a four-year course at the Hartt School. Davis had found the chords strange and had no idea what they were but thought that 'they still made some kind of sense to me.' Jackie told him he had 'got all the stuff happening' and then said, 'Where's your mother? We need to go and have a talk with mom!'

'Before we left the room,' wrote Davis, 'Mr. McLean noticed I had been looking at what I thought was the rather impressive skyline of downtown Hartford, Connecticut. He pointed out the window and said, "I know. It's a cow pasture. It's not New York, but there's a lot happening here at the University and in the city of Hartford. We have the Artists Collective, too. I think you'd do very well here for four years."'

He asked Davis if he'd like to study with Curtis Fuller, which is a bit like asking a drama student if he'd like to study with Harold Pinter. Persuading Davis' mother after that was child's play and the student went on to be a member of Jackie's quintet on the road and in the recording studio and, in due course, a faculty member at Hartt, teaching, of course, jazz studies on the trombone. After he graduated in 1989 it was McLean who managed to secure his first gig for him with Art Blakey's Jazz Messengers and in 1992 he played in his first McLean quintet. Students like Davis and the many others who went on to become jazz soloists or teachers, or both, were the focus of McLean's thoughts during his last years at the beginning of the twenty-first century. But he was growing older and was aware that mortality was stalking him slowly, if surely.

Interviewed by Sue Terry he told her that he was missing friends who were no longer around, particularly Billy Higgins, one of his favourite drummers whose playing was always spot on in support of the front-line soloists and who had a big smile on his face whenever he sat behind his drums. He indicated that the Collective was going strong, so was the course at the university and he could afford to sit back a bit and let it develop under its own momentum. His focus now was on going out on gigs and playing jazz with old and new students. At last he had time for some live playing even if record dates were not exactly pouring in. And he had reached a stage now where he could ask for, demand even, a fair payment for a night's music in a club. That was the sort of security he had earned, at last, with his academic work and his consistently high quality recordings.

He had a university department named after him, jazz clubs in Japan bearing his name and even an avenue in Hartford to be called Jackie McLean Avenue. Achievement on several levels but, his first love, playing jazz was still paramount. So if he slowed down and did a little less in the university and took only the gigs that paid well, who could blame him? He had paid all his dues and then some.

As for record dates Jackie was complaining to journalist Willard Jenkins in *Jazz Times*, as late as December 1996, that he was not being offered enough money to record and that record companies were offering recording contracts to young musicians, newly out of music colleges and ignoring established people like Grachan Moncur and many other fine players 'that have been out here for years and are just not getting a chance to record and get exposed.' Jackie thought that he had fallen into that group. 'I'm not going to accept that,' he told Jenkins. 'They can't pick up the phone and call me and ask me to do a record date for some silly little money and offer me crumbs. I've recorded for nothing already.'

When Jenkins asked him if record companies found him too demanding, he bristled, saying, 'It's always going to be like this.' He had played in many great bands, had great experiences and developed so many wonderful young musicians that it was surprising to him that record companies were not offering recording opportunities to him and his students.

It is, of course, a dilemma that seems unlikely ever to be resolved. However good the music, however gifted the soloists and musicians in the band, if the record companies can't sell a million copies and make a fortune on each one they record, they are just not interested. Only a very few big names and those who dilute their music with a large dose of pop, rock or other commercial attributes, will make it through.

Ultimately, the Jackie McLean story is one of success and considerable achievement against all the odds. Lester Young and Charlie Parker made it as musicians but did not have long, successful careers and a sustaining home life. Jackie did. And he made the most of it, living life to the full in every sense. If his teaching was intended initially as a means to subsidize earnings and provide a barrier against the precarious life of a working jazz musician, it turned out to be a major achievement in the long run, enhancing his already considerable reputation as he became a college professor of stature as well as a major soloist.

Some people may look on the long, hard years he spent addicted to heroin as being counterproductive and harmful, not to mention wasteful, but viewed from another angle it was something many jazz musicians went through in the 1940s and up to the late 1960s. Few indeed of the major soloists of those eras were not affected. Not that Jackie ever felt the need or desire to regret those years. It was a phase he passed through and something he seems to have accepted as a sort of 'education'. 'The first thing is I didn't get involved with drugs because of any particular person,' he told Spellman in the 1960s.[3] Nobody made him use them, he continued, and nobody influenced him to use them. He showed a certain naivety that would probably not apply these days when he said that people used drugs then because 'you've got to get burnt before you know what fire is,' and he thought it was just something else that adults didn't want high school kids to do. He didn't know it was harmful, didn't even know that heroin came from opium, he said, and he never had access to the literature about it that is available today or had anybody try to warn him or discourage him from using, 'trying to help the kids to stay away like they do today'. That just wasn't happening, he claimed, and he had thought 'It was just another way of getting high, like drinking or smoking pot.'

Sensibly, Jackie talked about liking the high he got from heroin in the beginning but then admitted that it took over the whole 'mind, body and life'. He loved the relaxation it gave him but gradually came to see that although he had thought that it made him play better, 'you find out later that you were *just* relaxed.' No end product. He realised, late but not too late, that the relaxation no longer helped him create meaningful solos, if it ever had. He needed to be stimulated from within, he told Spellman. 'It didn't do anything for me except teach me a long hard lesson.' He has also gone on record in scathing terms condemning the 'experts', the 'do-gooders', and anybody that classes addicts as worthless people or criminals. In Jackie's view they should have been forced to take the stuff, those people who thought it was just in the mind and you could get off it easily with willpower.

McLean was never apologetic in any way about his use of drugs. Over the years he was outspoken about the harm that heroin does. His addiction gave him a harsh, bitterly cruel lesson but one that he used to the advantage of many others when he was finally, irrevocably free it.

After he recorded *Nature Boy* Jackie headed confidently towards the twenty-first century, fit and healthy, keeping a master's eye on the progress and nurture of his students at both Hartford institutions and concentrating on taking the best of the live gigs offered to him or those that were self-generated at the Collective. If time was catching up with him and he was starting to slow down he showed no visible signs of it as the new century dawned although his recording career had effectively ended.

27

FAREWELL: THREE

The 1990s had been a very busy time for Jackie and particularly so as he had been able to go back to his first love, playing straight-ahead jazz in the clubs, at festivals in the USA and Europe and at his own Artists Collective venues. The latter often afforded an opportunity for him to invite old pals from the Blue Note days: musicians like Cedar Walton, Billy Higgins until his death in the early part of the decade, and trumpeter Donald Byrd. He became a regular at the Dizzy Gillespie memorial celebrations at the Blue Note club in New York and helped to bring in a cheery jazz Christmas for many years at the Village Vanguard with Walton and Higgins. As Gary Giddins reported in the June 2006 *Jazz Times* magazine, he was introduced by Sonny Rollins one year 'and damned if he didn't steal the evening with two specialities 'Solar' and 'Cottage for Sale'.'

An idea of how active he was during these later years of his life can be gained by noting that in 1994 he played in a concert at Carnegie Hall in NYC celebrating fifty years of Verve Records. He also played a concert alongside Sonny Rollins and worked on the Public Broadcasting TV channel's *Jazz* programmes. In 1995 he took a band made up of former students into the Village Vanguard, championing his young and not so young charges from the past in much the same way as he had always done. It was a long distance to the Vanguard in 1995 from his first leader date on records in 1955 when he had employed young, relatively unknown musicians like Ronald Tucker, Doug Watkins and Donald Byrd, but the principle was still the same. A gig at the

Vanguard in 1995 would most likely have brought in far more customers and revenue with Cedar Walton and a top professional section but that was not the way Jackie worked. If a special rhythm section was needed for a particular project, like the *Nature Boy* record date, it was a one-off occasion and certainly not a week-long gig at a prestigious jazz club.

During the last years of McLean's life, his fame as a musician and jazz soloist was greater in Japan than in his homeland. This is something that always surprised and amused him and he made many trips to play there, always receiving a huge ovation at the end of concerts. He was reported as walking along a Yokohama street one day on a playing trip when he spotted a small nightclub with the name: The Jackie McLean Coffee House. Much amused and flattered, he entered and found that the walls of the building were lined with the covers of practically every LP he had ever made. He made himself known to the owner and later went back to jam there with local jazz musicians. The willingness to jam is something that marked him out as special in much the same way as Charlie Parker, the man he was inextricably linked with all through his career as an alto saxophonist.

As for recognition and appreciation of his work, although the honour of the Japanese coffee house probably pleased as well as amused him, I suspect that being appreciated in his own country meant a lot more to him. On April 2nd 2001 he received the Beacon of Jazz Award from the New School university's Jazz and Contemporary Music Program in New York City and the following year he received recognition as a Jazz Master by the National Endowment for the Arts. 2002 also saw him inducted into the *DownBeat* magazine 'Jazz Education Hall of Fame'. In 2007, one year after his death, he was postumously awarded an honorary doctorate of music at the University of Hartford, one of the first people to receive honorary degrees from the university. The awards that came in his lifetime must have been very gratifying but perhaps Professor McLean might have given a wry smile and wondered why he had still, up until very recently, been receiving offers of nightclub and recording work for a pittance. Puzzling indeed. Not that he needed to worry by that time; he could take them or leave them and, as he often pointed out, he mostly left them. When he accepted gigs that were for less than the money he thought he was entitled to, it was always for good reasons. In the 1990s he played at the Village Vanguard frequently and described it as a 'homecoming'. He also took a band of young musicians into these gigs to give them exposure and, if the money was not quite what he was used to, it was at least drawing attention to him and his musicians.

'I'm knocked out going into the Village Vanguard,' he told a *New York Times* reporter, 'I worked there opposite Thelonious Monk and I really like Max Gordon, the club's owner.' He added that more than anything he was happy to be coming home to play. I believe it was very important to Jackie to renew his roots in New York in the 1990s and during the first two or three years of the twenty-first century. The Artists Collective was well established with new premises and other teachers who could carry on the good work, and he was free to get back to what he ultimately did best – play stunningly inventive jazz solos on alto saxophone. He pointed out that the Collective's music programme was now a full degree programme, so it was time for him to concentrate on playing again.

'I've always wanted to be remembered as something more than a saxophone player,' he told the *New York Times* correspondent Peter Watrous in 1990, but he knew that whatever else he did and however worthy and important it was, it could never fully take the place of standing in front of an audience and blowing his horn. He also, in that interview, reminisced about the past, mentioning that 'growing up in Harlem was incredible. My godfather played saxophone in the church ensemble at the Abyssinian Baptist Church... and I'd sit there and listen.' He finished by talking about the importance of that church for its connection to his past life.

His sound, his styling and his ability to play piercing, inventive jazz solos was not diminished even during the last years of his life. In an obituary in the *Guardian* newspaper,[1] critic John Fordham wrote that his later recordings suggested the edge of his playing was softening and the repertoire becoming more uneven but this is a view that few if any others seem to have shared. We have only to listen to the intensity and invention to be heard on the Triloka records and the high quality of the ballad playing on *Nature Boy* to refute this suggestion. And as it says on the *Everything2* internet site: 'Not true. Those who knew McLean knew he was a perfectionist who was demanding of others but much more so of himself. He often spoke of the importance of playing well, "as if it were your last solo".'[2]

Inevitably the time came, sometime in the early years of the new century, for McLean to play his last solo and we can be pretty certain that he played it well. He would never put in a second rate performance or give less than his very best. He died aged seventy-four on March 31st 2006 in Hartford. In his end was also his beginning as his body was returned to the famous Abyssinian Baptist church in Harlem. Dollie McLean said: 'Jackie left us very quietly and very peacefully, at home, surrounded by his wife and children. He gave so much in his life that he's still very much in our spirits and always will be.' The Revd. Calvin O. Butts said to the McLean family, 'I'm so glad you brought him home.'

At the funeral service Butts eulogised McLean and recalled that his godfather, Chief Norman Cobbs had given Jackie one of his first instruments, a soprano saxophone. Cobbs had played sax at the church when the famous Adam Clayton Powell had been pastor. The Abyssinian church was full to overflowing for the funeral service with over a thousand people in attendance. The service lasted ninety minutes and among those in mourning were trumpeter Freddie Hubbard, the player who had given such strong support on *Bluesnik* back in the 1960s, as well as educator and veteran pianist Billy Taylor, saxophonist Gene Ghee, pianist Larry Willis, drummer Warren Smith, bassist Nat Reeves and trombonist Steve Davis – the last three were Jackie's students and later band-mates at one time or another.

A large contingent of people from Hartford, where Jackie was so well-known and respected, came in by car or bus. Hartford's city treasurer thanked Jackie for 'the thousands of children whose lives he saved'. The Revd. Butts said that 'There was something deep in Jackie that caused him to spread his love through his music... there is evidence of stewardship. A legacy we can look at, study and learn.' Then saxophonist Jimmy Heath played Thelonious Monk's 'Round Midnight' and vocalist Eunice Newkirk sang 'Amazing Grace'. There were also several recordings by Jackie McLean played as part of the service.

Jackie finally came to rest in peace at Woodlawn Cemetery in the Bronx.

28

THE LEGACY: ONE
THE RECORDS

A lasting legacy of Jackie McLean will be, of course, the continuing work of the Artists Collective and the jazz department at the University of Hartford. He was responsible for starting both, and his continued work over more than two decades ensured their permanence. Then, of course, there are the recordings. The list is considerable and as good, complete discographies can be found on the internet very easily, I will content myself with pointing in the direction of those discs I consider to be the best and including those few that are, in my opinion, essential.

Monuments was Jackie's only really commercial record where he plays solos over a funk and fusion band backing. The individual solos are reasonably good and inventive, perhaps because he was incapable of playing a bad solo, but the band is not his bag, he does not sound comfortable with it and judging by his own words at various times, he couldn't have been happy with it. Not playing music like that.

The others I mention are all important although, as with all jazz musicians, some are better than others. Because jazz releases on disc are sporadic and come and go with different labels and numbers, I am sticking to the initial release labels and numbers, mostly, of course, original LP release but all of the records can be traced and supplied through specialist jazz record shops. And both LP and CDs can be found to buy or up for auction on internet sites. Where a particular record is considered very special or essential, I have marked it with an asterisk*.

The Miles Davis Sextet disc, originally issued as *Dig* (Prestige PRLP 7012), is well worth having, as much if not more for the work of Davis and Sonny Rollins as the very young Jackie Mac. And it was McLean's first jazz disc.

The two Blue Notes, *Miles Davis Vol 1* (1501) and *Vol 2* (1502) should not be overlooked and they offer splendid early bop from the beginning of the 1950s with Miles, J. J. Johnson, Horace Silver and Kenny Clarke, all playing very well although not all together as separate sessions were utilized. Jackie is in good, Parker-inspired form on the tracks that feature him. His individuality is just beginning to show in that hard, almost vinegary tone but it isn't developed strongly at this stage and he is still leaning heavily on Charlie Parker for solo inspiration.

Jackie's first major gig with the George Wallington Quintet is represented by the live set recorded for Progressive and later issued on Prestige: *Quintet at the Bohemia* (Progressive LP 1001 and Prestige PR 7820).

The saxophonist's first LP as a leader (*Jackie McLean Quintet*, 1955) is 'a must have' for any serious enthusiast if only because it finds the young altoist in exuberant, swinging, hard bopping form and brings in his first batch of young buddies in Donald Byrd, Mal Waldron, Doug Watkins and drummer (whatever happened to?) Ronald Tucker (Ad Lib 6601 or Jubilee 1064). This fine session is available on various labels at the time of writing including a CD which offers it with the full contents of a slightly later McLean-led session.

Two sessions recorded in January 1956 should be acquired by enthusiasts. The first (*Lights Out*) he made for Prestige, on PRLP 7035, with Donald Byrd, Elmo Hope on piano and Doug Watkins on bass. Tucker was replaced by Art Taylor and this proved to be a steady, often used bass and drum partnership from that point onwards. The other LP was the remarkable

Pithecanthropus Erectus on Atlantic 1237* by the Charles Mingus Jazz Workshop and this is an essential album.

The July 1956 Prestige date *4, 5 and 6* (PRLP 7048) is worth seeking out as it features a long and lyrical reading of 'Sentimental Journey' with Jackie at the top of his early style in his solo. 'Sentimental' brings out his best at this time and his blues-inflected, rich yet still somewhat strident tone. *Jackie's Pal* (PRLP 7068) pairs McLean with Bill Hardman on trumpet and it is illuminating to hear the contrast between their respective playing styles. This disc features a strong rhythm section with Mal Waldron on piano, Paul Chambers on bass and Philly Joe Jones on drums making his last recording for Prestige following a bitter disagreement with Bob Weinstock, the proprietor of that company.

In December 1956, Art Blakey brought his newly formed Jazz Messengers into the Columbia studios to tape *Hard Bop** (CL 1040). The disc, with slashing solos from Jackie, Hardman and Blakey, could almost have served as a demonstration disc for the new hard bop style just coming in at that time. 'Stella by Starlight' positively burns up the grooves but there is an exceptional emotional charge to all the solos and Blakey is magnificent from start to finish. This is the first LP where Jackie's strident, although highly lyrical sound, is fully realised. These five really put the 'hard' into hard bop. If there had been any lingering residue of Jackie playing like Charlie Parker and sounding just like him at times, this session is where he jettisoned most of Bird's phrases and began building dark, muscular alto sounds of his own.

As stated in Chapter 6 above, *A Long Drink of the Blues** on New Jazz (8253) is a very good McLean disc with one side taken up by an extended jam session and the other offering some superb examples of ballad playing by Jackie and his rhythm section.

Jackie McLean Plays Fat Jazz (Jubilee JLP 1093) has Webster Young on trumpet and the impressive young tuba soloist Ray Draper. This recording can be obtained along with Jackie's first leader date on Ad Lib on CD: *The Complete Jubilee Sessions* (Lonehill Jazz LHJ 10269).

Not to be missed at any price is Sonny Clark's leader date *Cool Struttin'** (Blue Note BLP 1588) from January 5th 1958. This is one of those supercharged Blue Note hard bop dates where everybody is on top form. The rhythm section of Clark, Paul Chambers and Philly Joe Jones is as good as you could possibly get in 1958 and they play with style, relish and the sort of swing that only the very best musicians can muster. Art Farmer and Jackie are both flying high and the opening title blues is a real beauty. It is also worth seeking out the previously unissued *Cool Struttin' Vol 2* (Blue Note 1592) which the Japanese King company put out in the 1980s and it continued to appear with releases from Toshiba EMI from that country. It has two tracks from the session with Jackie and Farmer and three from another session with Kenny Burrell on guitar and Pete LaRoca at the drums.

1959 saw Jackie move to Blue Note to record, and the start of arguably the most productive few years of his recorded output. It began with the magnificent *Jackie's Bag*, one half featuring a smouldering rhythm section of Sonny Clark, piano, Chambers and Jones and the others, recorded a year later, with Kenny Drew and Art Taylor and the splendid but hopelessly underrated Tina Brooks on tenor sax and Blue Mitchell on trumpet. It may have taken over a year for this LP to be completed but the finished result made it well worth the wait.

On February 4th 1959, McLean was part of an all-star lineup for bassist Charles Mingus' *Blues and Roots* on Atlantic LP 1305. Although the disc was not fully representative of what Jackie was doing in early 1959, it is indicative of the way modern jazz was developing in that crucial year, one aspect of developments that included Miles Davis and his essential *Kind of Blue* LP and Dave Brubeck with his time signature experiments on *Take Five*. And Jackie does play some cracking, advanced sounding solos.

Blue Note BLP 4013, which was issued with the title *New Soil*, was the first indication that he was looking for new means of expression and seeking to expand his solo capabilities. It featured Walter Davis who was chosen later for the keyboard duties on the important *Let Freedom Ring* album. Donald Byrd was on trumpet and the drummer on this album, Pete LaRoca, would also feature on another, very important future McLean Blue Note session.

Donald Byrd was the leader on *Fuego* (Blue Note BLP 4026)* on October 4th 1959. The partnership between McLean and Byrd was never better or more inspired-sounding than on this sparkling set with strong contributions from Duke Pearson on piano, Doug Watkins, and drummer Lex Humphries who had seen service in the Dizzy Gillespie band. With the repertory system adopted by Blue Note in the 1960s, musicians became sidemen for their friends and colleagues as well as leaders and Jackie often shone brightly on other people's dates: this was certainly one of them.

Swing, Swang, Swingin' on Blue Note 4024 is McLean's set of quality standards, with one blues at the end, showing beyond all reasonable doubt that he was a consummate interpreter of ballads by this time. Walter Bishop, the upcoming Jimmy Garrison and Art Taylor furnish the steady support.

The Music From the Connection (Blue Note 4027)* is yet another essential McLean purchase for anybody new to his music. Pianist Redd wrote music that fits this session like a glove and he and McLean play it with spirit throughout, aided and abetted by Michael Mattos on bass and Larry Ritchie on drums, two musicians who played on many of the theatre presentations.

Two Blue Note releases from April 1960 are well worthy of consideration. *Capuchin Swing* (BLP 4038) came out under

McLean's name and *Lee-Way* (BLP 4043) was issued under the leadership of Lee Morgan. The Morgan disc is notable for four extended tracks with strong solos from Morgan and McLean and explosive, supportive drumming by Art Blakey. It is like a reunion of the mid-1950s Messengers with Paul Chambers the only non-Messenger on board.

Freddie Redd's *Shades of Redd* on BLP 4045 should not be overlooked and neither should Donald Byrd's *Byrd in Flight* on BLP 4048, both recorded in the summer of 1960.

Blue Note 4067* is the number of *Bluesnik*, Jackie's blues and hard bop masterpiece and this one should be acquired at all costs. These basic blues tracks have a particular magic that will only become apparent when you listen to the record. Freddie Hubbard is in sparkling form and so is Kenny Drew on piano, Pete LaRoca, and the bass player Jackie used whenever he could, Doug Watkins. This was to be the last occasion as Watkins died a few months later.

October 26th 1961 was the date when McLean recorded with trumpeter Tommy Turrentine and the fine rhythm section of Sonny Clark, Butch Warren and Billy Higgins for *A Fickle Sonance* (BLP 4089)*. In November of that year Jackie had linked up with trumpeter Kenny Dorham and the quintet they toured with recorded *Inta Somethin'* (Pacific Jazz PJ 41) under Kenny's leadership at the Jazz Workshop in San Francisco.

Jackie McLean's move into modal and more free style jazz began, on records at least, with *Let Freedom Ring* on BLP 4106.* This set represented not just the first steps into new, freer, experimental music; it was also one of Jackie's very best single LP programmes. The striking 'Melody for Melonae' and the intense lyricism of 'I'll Keep Loving You' were just the beginning. All four extended tracks bear repeated auditions and, in my opinion, never lose their considerable musical appeal. Jackie's horn is strident and deep blue but his phrases are more wild and seemingly abandoned although careful study reveals that he is in full control at all times. The frequent time signature changes, the occasional high pitched shrieks and squeals and the way he fashions each melody and variations on it all indicate a major inventive soloist exploring new ground and producing fresh, challenging music. The rhythm section must have been chosen with great care as the leader would have been aware of the pitfalls of trying to play in the 'new thing' free jazz style with a conventional section set in its ways. So he picked Walter Davis on piano who had shown an aptitude for producing something fresh and different in the studio. Bassist Herbie Lewis was just twenty years old at the time and had worked with adventurous spirits like Harold Land, Dupree Bolton and Elmo Hope. McLean was already familiar with Billy Higgins as a flexible, hard swinging drummer and his pedigree, working with Ornette Coleman, was impeccable. With these seasoned but still young musicians, Jackie produced one of his best and certainly his most adventurous set to date. No serious jazz collection should be without this disc and *Bluesnik*.

Three other discs from 1962 may not be essential but they are very good and should be sought out. Another session with Kenny Dorham's quintet (although it was dual leadership on the road at the time) produced *Matador* (United Artists UAJ 14007). Then there were two excellent Blue Note LPs made, I believe, as back-ups in case the new free style did not take: *Hipnosis* on Blue Note BN LA 483-H2 was also issued in Japan as a single record titled *The Jackie McLean Quintet* (BLP 4116). The quartet date *Tippin' the Scales* (BST 84427) also first came out as a Japanese Blue Note (GXF 3062). These two LPs represent the best of, for want of a better expression, the old Jackie McLean, and what he would have gone on sounding like if he had kept to the style he began with in the late 1940s. Fortunately he was forever striving, pushing boundaries and never tired of searching out the new. And yet these samples of his 'old' music are extremely valuable and some of the best modern jazz (bop style) put on record.

Vertigo on Blue Note LT 1085 from 1963 did not make it to the shops until many years later but the real treasure of that year was *One Step Beyond* (BLP 4037)*. All the tracks, 'Frankenstein', 'Saturday and Sunday', 'Blue Rondo' and 'Ghost Town' have a strange, other worldly feel with the music episodic, occasionally brilliant in individual solos but mostly a collective set of new wave style improvisations. 'Ghost Town' is particularly spooky with Tony Williams' drums tracing a suitably haunting set of patterns. Jackie had come up with a successful whole new style of music, consolidated by this release. His own playing had obviously gone through a change by this time; whereas *Let Freedom Ring* had been experimental and a signpost to the new Jackie, this release had him confidently embracing long, colourful lines where he swooped down into the lower register freely, played occasional sour notes, varied the tempo or let out high pitched but carefully planned squeals. It wasn't comparable to what Ornette Coleman was doing but it was a new and invigorating variation on McLean solos and the freshness of his approach and execution produced totally absorbing music.

Destination – Out from September 1963 is almost as good, in the same free-flowing style and with similar personnel although the bass is taken over by Larry Ridley and Roy Haynes is on drums. Blue Note BLP 4165 is the number and it is not to be overlooked.

1964 saw the release of *It's Time* (Blue Note BLP 4179), with Charles Tolliver in the trumpet role he would occupy frequently with Jackie for some time. The 1980s-issued *Tom Cat* (Blue Note LT 1058), a 1964 Lee Morgan record, features Jackie extensively and is well worth adding to record collections. *Action* (BLP 4218) was the last McLean LP in that year and a good one.

The best of 1965 is represented, I feel, by *Right Now* on BLP 4215 and another Lee Morgan-led session *Cornbread* (BLP 4222).

Both are very good and the Morgan album represents his attempt to move into more free, contemporary areas of expression although it is not as full-ahead and style changing as McLean's music of the time.

The collaboration with Ornette Coleman, with the joint leader playing trumpet and violin is an essential record even if it misses several chances to present a more balanced view of what both leaders were doing at the time. An alto duet or two between the men who represented the best of modern alto, old and new, at that time, would have been great. So, an opportunity missed, even more so when you consider that pianist Cecil Taylor was also scheduled to appear. Even with all its shortcomings though, *New and Old Gospel* (Blue Note BLP 4262)* is not to be missed.

The late 1960s represents a slightly uneven patch in Jackie's discography, possibly because he was just starting to focus more of his time and attention on human rights issues and teaching and counselling. Not very much really stands out from this period but he plays well on the Jack Wilson Sextet disc, *Easterly Winds* (BST 84270). A Hank Mobley session, *Hi Voltage* on BST 84273, is another record worth tracking down, with a sterling cast of musicians including Blue Mitchell on trumpet and Billy Higgins on drums. Some rejected Blue Note masters at this period suggest that McLean's attention was not always fully focused on the recording studios.

There is a complete lack of recording activity from July 1968 until August 1972 and this period coincides, of course, with the move to Hartford and the setting up and first workings of the jazz department he founded at the university. After that there were several trips to the continent of Europe and opportunities to play and record with other American jazz musicians and locals there. In Denmark he recorded with Gary Bartz, Lee Konitz, Charlie Mariano and a Danish rhythm section on an 'altissimo jam session' and he also linked up with tenor man Dexter Gordon on more than one occasion. He played frequently at this time at the famous Jazzhus Montmartre in Copenhagen, usually with a rhythm section comprising American pianist Kenny Drew, Danish bassist and drummer, Niels-Henning Ørsted Pedersen and Alex Riel. How he managed to fit in all these trips to Europe, play in clubs and get the university jazz course up and running is anybody's guess. It must have taken great stamina and dedication to say the least.

In the 1970s there were recording sessions in NYC as well as Tokyo, Japan and a set with the Great Jazz Trio: Hank Jones, piano, Ron Carter, bass, and Tony Williams on drums. There were trips back to Japan in the 1980s and an increase in recording activity. One record stands out from this period, *Dynasty* on Triloka 477181*, recorded in 1988. Billed as the Jackie McLean–Rene McLean Quintet, it features father and son in exultant form with ex-students Nat Reeves on bass, Hotep Idris Galeta on piano and Carl Allen at the drums. The nine fiery tracks on this CD are not to be missed, with a roaring 'Five', a sensuous ballad reading of 'A House Is Not a Home' and the wild 'J. Mac's Dynasty'. This disc has all the fire and fervour of the best of the early Blue Notes and is a good, 'sound' example of what Jackie was doing through all those years of teaching and training student musicians.

Another pair of records well worth having are the two *Tribute to Charlie Parker: Volume One* on Verve 841 132-2 and *Volume Two* on Verve 841 133-2. Recorded in France in 1989 these discs are also listed as Birdology 37014 in that country but *Don Sickler–Jackie McLean Septet* is the most familiar title. With veterans of Parker's famous combos like Jordan and Haynes and contemporaries like Cecil Payne on board, it would be hard to find a better lineup for a Parker tribute. From the first notes of 'Bird Lives' on volume one you can tell that all these musicians are up for a tribute to the Bird. Only Don Stickler's cool, burnished trumpet is somewhat out of synchronisation with the Parker bop ambience on the disc; not his fault, he is from a different generation and unlike Payne, Griffin, Jordan, Haynes and McLean, he didn't live through the bop scene at its height. Jackie is, as you might expect, on absolutely top form here, charging through the familiar Parker classics with his own mix of bop, blues and free playing that became indelibly etched into his musical personality. The version here of 'Parker's Mood' is just about the last word on this famous blues. McLean's inspired, passionate solo is, surely, the one Charlie Parker himself would have loved to have played. Like his hero before him, however, he is always instantly recognisable as his own man. This session consolidated his love and respect for Parker's music with everything he had absorbed over the thirty-four years that had elapsed since Parker's death. Inspiring each other perhaps, everybody plays at the top of their abilities on this disc, making it a fitting tribute to the bop master.

A good example of the musical plateau that Jackie had reached by the 1990s can be heard on the Birdology release *Rhythm of the Earth* (1992) on FDM 37009-2 where he demonstrates musically his newly discovered 'Sirius System' and plays with rare intensity and commitment for a musician aged sixty. This was a highly contemporary jazz disc and the band boasted names like trumpeter Roy Hargrove and vibraphone master Steve Nelson. All the musicians play with spirit and plenty of skill and all, except Hargrove and Nelson, are ex-students of the leader's.

McLean was sixty-eight when he went into the studios in NYC to record *Nature Boy* in June 1999 but you wouldn't know it. Initially released on the Japanese Somethin' Else label (TOCJ 68045)*, it proved to be his last commercially released recording. Later, it was released as a Blue Note CD and it is, surprisingly perhaps, one of Jackie's best ever records, easily standing alongside some of his classic early Prestige and Blue Note discs when he was approaching his prime as a soloist. A set of eight sterling ballads played with variation of tempos and strong, lyric warmth and conviction. He couldn't have chosen a better, more sympathetic rhythm section at that time and the record will stand as a superb swan song. Most jazz musicians who reach the age of sixty-five or over are going through the motions or playing badly or not at all. Jackie proved that he could still play to the highest standards and produce moving music right to the very end.

29

THE LEGACY: TWO

When Jackie was asked in 1976 how he felt about being a legend by an interviewer in the film *Jackie McLean on Mars*, he did not answer the question; he said instead that he felt like 'an exploited poor musician'. That was how he felt after twenty-six years as a professional musician and a major, distinguished jazz soloist. It was not the same for the other part of his life where he spent many satisfying hours instructing young students and small children in the classrooms of the University of Hartford and at his own Artists Collective. The documentary film shows him listening to a very small girl playing the flute and encouraging and helping her with her interpretation. Another shot focuses on him talking to a class of students about how John Coltrane's music altered over the years and the way his playing changed and developed. This side of his career was obviously very satisfying to him and he felt that he was rewarded for his efforts artistically and financially.

As he said on other occasions, he had to worry about paying his bills and after he started teaching at Hartford and with the Collective, he no longer had that worry to contend with. He found a way to play whenever he wanted to and whenever gigs were available, and teach too on a regular basis, but it is more than unfortunate, to put it mildly, that he rarely felt able to earn a living wage as a musician. His daughter Melonae described her father not only working at almost all the NYC jazz clubs but initiating the music policy in some of them.[1] Slugs Saloon, formerly an Armenian bar, became a top jazz venue with most of the giants of jazz in the 1960s performing there. Jackie had started the jazz sessions, proposing Sunday afternoon sessions for his band and, once these were established and successful, the owners had extended their policy to jazz every night of the week. But for McLean there were the problems arising from his addiction to heroin in the 1960s. When he lost his cabaret card he lost most of the opportunities for a musician to earn a living. He later admitted that he had taken club jobs, performing as John Lenwood, using his middle name as an alias. He said in 1976 that it was the loss of that card that prompted him to look into the possibilities of other work. Early experience with young offenders was a beginning, once he had finally kicked his own habit.

He was a good man, somebody who would help other people instinctively and not for financial gain. The very opposite of mercenary, in fact. Melonae tells the story of a cab driver, on the verge of suicide due to his drug addiction, who came into contact with Jackie and today credits him with saving his life.[2] She also tells of a Japanese man who visited Hartford to hear McLean play and to meet him. In his youth he had travelled from a remote area of the country to hear Jackie play in Tokyo. Having arrived in Hartford he ran out of money and Jackie gave him a meal and enough money to get back home. He became an executive at a Japanese automobile company and these stories help to keep the former 'Little Melonae' connected to her father.[2]

It is difficult to accept that somebody as talented and as caring a person as he was should have had to spend a large proportion of his time scuffling for poorly paid gigs and almost as badly paid record dates. The last part of the film *Jackie McLean on Mars* shows him lecturing a student class on the abysmal lack of appreciation of jazz in the American media and in the country generally. He urges the students to promote the music forcefully and not be sucked into playing poor quality music for large monetary rewards. The problem, of course, is that jazz has never had a good press or been promoted on radio and television or newspapers either in the United States or in the UK. While popular music of every shade and description is given plenty of coverage in the respective media outlets, jazz is treated like the poor relation. The argument is that commercial radio and television companies, and newspapers for that matter, have to depend on advertisers and the profits they provide for their shareholders. They are therefore obliged only to present music that is 'pop' or rock or has some kind of universal appeal. This argument does have some justification but not much and hardly excuses complete disregard for a quality music that is loved by a minority of enthusiasts all over the world. And there is absolutely no excuse for the BBC in Britain who only broadcast two or three hours a week on radio with little or nothing on television when they are a public service broadcaster, receiving millions of pounds in licence fees to provide diverse entertainment for the entire population. Clearly they are not doing their job. Clearly they do not care one way or the other.

It is nearly forty years since Jackie McLean made his comments about the media ignoring jazz and very little, if anything, has changed since then. He refers in the film to a morning television show for children that focused on ragtime music and included 'The Entertainer' and many other compositions but never once mentioned composer Scott Joplin. In another segment in which he is seen lecturing students passionately on the same theme, he is scathing about fellow musicians Lou Donaldson and Donald Byrd, both heavily into funk and fusion music at the time. Jackie urged his students to listen to Donaldson's early jazz records and to judge him on those and he made the point that he felt sure that neither he nor Byrd were smiling when they played their current commercial music. Referring to Byrd he said, 'he can't be, not playing that music.' What remained unspoken was the reason they were playing 'that music'. Money. Lots of it. Without seeking to make vast amounts, McLean found a way to make a good living by combining work as an educator with concert and club dates whenever he could fit them in. And he never compromised or diluted his music to give it mass appeal.

A point jazz enthusiasts often make when they get together is that theirs is a minority music with limited appeal so they can't expect much in the way of media coverage and public acceptance. And yet, as Jackie McLean pointed out to his students, people know and like what they see and hear. They know Alice Cooper because they see him frequently but they don't know Thelonious Monk. In the UK people know Robbie Williams and Liam Gallagher but they don't know pianist Gwilym Simcock or saxophonist Alan Barnes, both superb musicians. How different would that be if the BBC broadcast three or four extra hours of jazz every week from now on?

In addition to all his considerable accomplishments, Jackie McLean posed many questions about how jazz is perceived, presented and treated. His own response in terms of his playing and teaching was priceless but the answers to most of his searching questions are yet to be provided.

NOTES

Chapter 1: TIME WARP ONE: SITTING IN FOR THE BIRD
1. From *Jazz – A Film* by Ken Burns, 10 April 1996 including transcripts: *http://www.pbs.org/jazz/about/pdfs/McLean.pdf*, visited 3 March 2012.

Chapter 2: SUGAR HILL, HARLEM
1. *Jazz – A Film.*
2. A. B. Spellman, *Four Lives in the Bebop Business*, New York: Limelight, 1994, p.184.
3. Alyn Shipton, *A New History of Jazz*, London: Continuum, 2001, pp.652-3.

Chapter 3: OUT OF THE BLUE
1. Ira Gitler, notes, Prestige 7012.
2. *Jazz – A Film.*
3. A. B. Spellman, *Four Lives.*
4. *Jazz – A Film.*

Chapter 4: STARTING AS HE MEANT TO GO ON
1. Charlie Mack, notes, *The New Tradition*, Ad Lib AD 6601, 1955.

Chapter 5: ISN'T JACKIE McLEAN IN THERE SOMEWHERE?
1. *Pithecanthropus Erectus*, Atlantic 1237, 1956.
2. Will Thornbury, notes, *Dynasty*, Triloka Records 181-2, 1990.
3. Thornbury, *Dynasty.*
4. Thornbury, *Dynasty.*
5. Thornbury, *Dynasty.*
6. From Art Blakey and the Jazz Messengers, *Moanin'*, BLP 4003.

Chapter 6: THE JAZZ LIFE
1. *Jazz – A Film.*
2. *Jazz – A Film.*
3. *Jazz – A Film.*

Chapter 7: THE SHAPING OF A MAJOR SOLOIST
1. *Jazz – A Film.*
2. *Jazz – A Film.*
3. *Jazz – A Film.*
4. Thornbury, *Dynasty*; and *Jazz – A Film.*
5. *Jazz – A Film.*
6. *Blue Note: A Story of Modern Jazz*, DVD, Euroarts 2005678.

Chapter 8: BLUE NOTE BEGINNINGS
1. *Jazz Monthly*, December 1959, Vol 5, No 10.

Chapter 9: THE CONNECTION
1. *Jazz – A Film.*
2. For further discussion of the situation in the UK, see Peter King, *Flying High: A Jazz Life and Beyond*, London: Northway Publications, 2011, pp.104-9 and 128-30.
3. Bob Blumenthal, notes, *Jackie's Bag*, Blue Note BLP 4051, CD issue 42303.
4. Blue Note BLP 4067 and CDP 7 84067 2.

Chapter 11: NEW DIRECTIONS AND OLD STANDBYS
1. J. McLean, notes, *Let Freedom Ring*, Blue Note LP and CDP 7 46527.

Chapter 12: ONE STEP FORWARD, ONE STEP BACK
1. Michael James, 'A Progress Report on Jackie McLean', *Jazz Monthly*, 1962.

Chapter 13: ONE STEP BEYOND
1. *Jazz – A Film.*

Chapter 14: DESTINATION – OUT
1. *Jazz – A Film.*

Chapter 15: ACTION
1. A. B. Spellman, *Four Lives*.
2. *Jazz – A Film.*
3. Thomas Owens, *Bebop: The Music and its Players*, New York: OUP, 1996.
4. Stephen H. Lehman, 'McLean's Scene: Jackie McLean as

Improviser, Educator & Activist', *Critical Studies in Improvisation*, Vol 3, No 2, 2008, Columbia University.

Chapter 17: TEACHING
1. Lehman, 'McLean's Scene'.
2. *Jackie McLean on Mars*, a film by Ken Levis, 1979. See *http://kenlevis.com*, visited April 14, 2012
3. *Jazz – A Film*.
4. Lehman, 'McLean's Scene'.

Chapter 18: MUSICIAN, SOLOIST, EDUCATOR, ACTIVIST
1. *Jackie McLean on Mars*.
2. Lehman, 'McLean's Scene'.
3. Lehman, 'McLean's Scene'.

Chapter 19: THE ARTISTS COLLECTIVE
1. Matt Schudel, obituary of Jackie McLean, *Washington Post*, April 2 2006.

Chapter 21: TIME WARP TWO: PARKER'S MOOD
1. Constructed from a conversation between McLean and Ken Burns in *Jazz – A Film*.

Chapter 22: RHYTHM OF THE EARTH
1. *Jazz – A Film*.

Chapter 23: WORKING MUSICIAN
1. Gary Giddins, *Jazz Times*, June 2006.
2. Alex Henderson, *http://www.allaboutjazz.com/php/article.php?id=2870*, visited 22 September 2011.

Chapter 24: THE SOUND OF JAZZ
1. Gary Giddins, *Weather Bird: Jazz at the Dawn of its Second Century*, New York: Oxford University Press, 2004, p.71.
2. Ira Gitler, notes to *A Fickle Sonance*, Blue Note 4089, 1961.

Chapter 25: TIME WARP THREE: FAREWELL ONE
1. Constructed from conversations in *Jazz – A Film*.

Chapter 26: FAREWELL TWO
1. Quoted by Chuck Obuchowski in 'One Step Beyond: Reflections of Jackie McLean', WWUH website, visited 10 April 2012: *http://www.wwuh.org/program/articles/julaug06/mclean.htm.*
2. Hartt School website, visited 10 April 2012: *http://harttweb.hartford.edu/admissions/choose/choosestudent.aspx* 2.
3. A. B. Spellman, *Four Lives.*

Chapter 27: FAREWELL THREE
1. John Fordham, *Guardian*, 3 April, 2006.
2. *http://everything2.com/title/jackie+mclean*, visited 3 March 2012.

Chapter 29: THE LEGACY: TWO
1. *Hog River Journal*, a magazine covering Connecticut history, Fall 2008.
2. *Hog River Journal.*

RECOMMENDED RECORDS

Classic jazz records are known by their original issue numbers, which I have used here. New CD releases come and go, catalogue numbers change and today, more than fifty years after recording, much of McLean's music is out of copyright and anybody can reissue it in any form they like, double, multiple CDs, etc. The most recent recordings were, of course, issued only as compact discs.

This is not a full discography but, rather, a list of recommended records with an asterisk for those considered to have special merit. It is not comprehensive, nor is it intended to be, but it is my selection of some of the best.

Miles Davis Sextet Vol 1, 1952, Blue Note 1501 and Vol 2, 1502.

George Wallington Quintet, *At the Café Bohemia*, 1955, Progressive LP 1001.

Jackie McLean Quintet, *The New Tradition*, 1955, Ad Lib 6601 and Jubilee JLP 1064.

Jackie McLean, *Lights Out*, 1956, Prestige PLP 7035.

Charles Mingus Quintet, *Pithecanthropus Erectus*, 1956, Atlantic 1237.*

Jackie McLean, *4, 5 and 6*, 1956, Prestige PRLP 7048.

Jackie McLean Quintet, *Jackie's Pal*, 1956, Prestige PRLP 7068.

Art Blakey and the Jazz Messengers, *Hard Bop*, 1956, Columbia CL 1040.

Jackie McLean Quartet, *A Long Drink of the Blues*, 1957, New Jazz NJLP 8253.

Art Blakey and the Jazz Messengers, *A Night in Tunisia*, 1957, Vik Lax 1115.* The Bluebird CD issue of this sterling session has three alternate takes including a sizzling extra 'Night In Tunisia', Bluebird 09026 63896-2.

Jackie McLean Sextet, *Jackie McLean Plays Fat Jazz*, 1957, Jubilee 1093.

Sonny Clark Quintet, *Cool Struttin'*, 1958, Blue Note 1588.* *Cool Struttin' Vol 2*, 1958, Blue Note 1592, only released in Japan (K18P 9297).

Donald Byrd Sextet, *Off to the Races*, 1958, Blue Note 4007.

Jackie McLean Quintet, *Jackie's Bag*, 1959, Blue Note 4051.*

Charles Mingus Nonet, *Blues and Roots*, 1959, Atlantic 1305.*

Jackie McLean Quintet, *New Soil*, 1959, Blue Note 4013.*

Donald Byrd Quintet, *Fuego*, 1959, Blue Note 4026.

Jackie McLean Quartet, *Swing, Swang, Swingin'*, 1959, Blue Note 4024.

Freddie Redd Quartet, *Music from the Connection*, 1960, Blue Note 4027.*

Jackie McLean Quintet, *Capuchin Swing*, 1960, Blue Note 4038.

Lee Morgan Quintet, *Lee-Way*, 1960, Blue Note 4034.

Donald Byrd Quintet, *Byrd in Flight*, 1960, Blue Note 4048.

Jackie McLean Sextet, *Jackie's Bag*, 1960, Blue Note 4051.*

Jackie McLean Quintet, *Bluesnik*, 1961, Blue Note 4067.*

Jackie McLean Quintet, *A Fickle Sonance*, 1961, Blue Note 4089.*

Kenny Dorham Quintet, *Inta Somethin'*, 1962, Pacific Jazz PJ 41.

Jackie McLean Quartet, *Let Freedom Ring*, 1962, Blue Note 4016.*

RECORD LIST

Jackie McLean Quartet, *Tippin' the Scales*, 1962, Blue Note Japan GXF 3062.*

Jackie McLean Quintet, *Vertigo*, 1962, Blue Note LT 1085.

Jackie McLean Quintet, *One Step Beyond*, 1963, Blue Note 4137.*

Jackie McLean Quintet, *Destination-Out*, 1963, Blue Note 4165.

Jackie McLean Quintet, *It's Time*, 1964, Blue Note 4179.*

Lee Morgan Sextet, *Tom Cat*, 1964, Blue Note LT 1058.

Jackie McLean Quintet, *Action*, 1964, Blue Note 4218.

Jackie McLean Quintet, *Right Now*, 1965, Blue Note 4215.

Lee Morgan Sextet, *Cornbread*, 1965, Blue Note 4222.

Jackie McLean Quintet, *Hipnosis*, 1962 and 1967, Blue Note LA 483-H2.*

Jackie McLean Quintet, *New and Old Gospel*, 1967, Blue Note 4262.

Jack Wilson Sextet, *Easterly Winds*, 1967, Blue Note 4270.

Jackie McLean Quintet, *One Night with Blue Note*, 1985, Blue Note BT 85114.

Jackie McLean Quintet, *Dynasty*, 1988, Triloka 477181.*

Jackie McLean Septet, *Tribute to Charlie Parker*, 1989, Birdology FDM 37014-2.

Jackie McLean Septet, *Rhythm of the Earth*, 1992, Birdology FDM 37009-2.

Jackie McLean Sextet, *Rites of Passage*, 1991, Triloka 477188.

Jackie McLean Quartet, *Somethin' Else*, 1999, Japan TOCJ 68045.*

INDEX

Abyssinian Baptist Church, 7, 174-5.
Ad Lib Records, 20-23, 38, 77, 178, 180.
Adderley, Julian 'Cannonball', 37, 142, 156.
Ali, Rashied, 117.
Allen, Carl, 133, 186.
Allen, Kris, 130.
American Federation of Musicians, 28.
Ammons, Gene, 20, 37, 44.
Armstrong, Louis, 90, 150.
Artists Collective, 123, 125-9, 145, 148, 152-3, 166-8, 171-2, 174, 177, 189.
Association for the Advancement of Creative Musicians, 125.
Atlantic Records, 43, 46, 59, 76, 92, 179-80.
Ayler, Albert, 144.
Bacharach, Burt, 134.
Barnes, Alan, 192.
Bartz, Gary, 132, 185.
Basie, Count, 6.
BBC, 191-2.
Berliner, Paul, 116.
Bird, the film, 141.
Birdland, 8, 10, 15-16, 29, 36, 164.
Birdology Records, 137, 145, 156, 186-7.

Bishop, Walter, Jr., 12, 14, 50, 57, 72, 75, 181.
Black Panthers, 103, 123.
Blakey, Art, 1-3, 12, 14-15, 21, 24, 29-32, 35, 37, 39-42, 47, 59, 78, 96, 109, 112, 114-5, 168, 179, 182.
 Jazz Messengers, 20, 24, 30, 35, 37, 39, 41, 47, 89, 109, 114-5, 168, 179, 182.
Blue Note Records, 14, 44-6, 48-50, 53-7, 59, 61, 65-8, 71-2, 75-7, 79, 85, 88-90, 92-3, 96, 98, 101, 104-5, 117-22, 132-3, 144, 153, 156-7, 172, 180-5, 187.
Blumenthal, Bob, 56, 63, 70, 102, 107.
Bolton, Dupree, 183.
Boplicity Records, 53.
Bowler, Phil, 152.
Bradshaw, Tiny, 7.
Briggs, Jimmy, 7-8.
Brooks, Tina, 53, 57, 180.
Brown, Garnett, 118.
Brubeck, Dave, 181.
Burns, Ken, 2, 6, 33, 36, 39, 79, 104, 113.
Burrell, Kenny, 180.
Burton, Abraham, 130, 156.
Butts, Rev. Calvin O., 175-6.
Byard, Jackie, 115.

Byrd, Donald, 20, 22-3, 25-6, 35, 37-8, 41, 45, 48, 61, 65, 77, 85, 88-9, 149, 166, 172-3, 178, 181-2, 191.

Café Bohemia, NYC, 22, 165.

Candid Records, 92.

Carnegie Hall, NYC, 172.

Carter, Benny, 155.

Carter, Ron, 132, 136, 186.

Catlett, Big Sid, 106.

Chambers, Paul, 22, 24, 35, 45, 48, 55, 57, 76, 78, 179-80, 182.

Clark, Sonny, 44-5, 55, 61, 64-5, 71, 73-5, 180, 182.

Clarke, Kenny, 14, 142, 178.

Clarke, Shirley, 95.

Cobb, Arnett, 5.

Cobbs, Norman, 7, 175.

Coggins, Gil, 14, 37.

Cole, Nat King, 5.

Coleman, Ornette, 27, 59, 63, 67, 72, 78, 85, 87, 89, 92, 95, 103, 106-9, 143-4, 183-5.

Coltrane, John, 24, 59, 61, 67, 69, 77-8, 90, 95, 103, 113, 121-2, 144, 153, 155, 159, 189.

Columbia Records, 56, 179.

Connection, The, play and film, 48, 51-6, 77, 80-2, 95, 110, 181.

Contemporary Records, 92.

Cooper, Alice, 192.

Coronet Club, NYC, 83, 89, 99.

Cranshaw, Bob, 44, 101-2, 118.

Davis, Miles, 8, 10, 12-15, 19, 21, 23-4, 34, 40-41, 44, 50, 56, 63-4, 67-8, 74, 77, 83, 85, 87-8, 90, 112-3, 115, 120, 153, 178, 181.

Davis, Steve, 145-6, 152, 167-8, 176.

Davis, Walter Jr., 48-9, 66, 69, 144, 181, 183.

DeBrest, Spanky, 30.

DeJohnette, Jack, 95, 105-6, 120-1.

DePalma, Don, 166.

DiRubbo, Mike, 130.

Dockery, Sam, 30.

Dogon people, 145.

Dolphy, Eric, 67, 89, 92, 101, 144.

Donaldson, Lou, 93, 191.

Dorham, Kenny, 30, 63, 66-7, 72-6, 182-3.

DownBeat magazine, 46, 157, 173.

Draper, Ray, 37-8, 180.

Drew, Kenny, 5, 8, 15, 29-30, 57, 59-61, 128, 132, 180, 182, 186.

DuQuette, Mike, 166.

Eastwood, Clint, 141.

Ellington, Duke, 5, 10, 67, 150.

Escoffery, Wayne, 130.

Evers, Medgar, 104.

Farmer, Art, 35, 44-5, 180.

Five Spot club, NYC, 152.

Fordham, John, 175.

Fuller, Curtis, 96, 168.

Galeta, Hotep Idris, 133, 135, 186.

Gallagher, Liam, 192.
Gardner, Barbara J., 157.
Garland, Judy, 36.
Garland, Red, 24.
Garrison, Jimmy, 50, 181.
Garvin, Michael, 132.
Gelber, Jack, 51-2, 54, 95.
Gershwin, George, 167.
Ghee, Gene, 175.
Giddins, Gary, 152, 156, 172.
Gillespie, Dizzy, 5-6, 18, 21, 23, 27, 67, 114, 142, 172, 181.
Gitler, Ira, 12-13, 58, 60, 64, 156.
Goldberg, Joe, 48-50.
Golson, Benny, 97.
Gordon, Dexter, 6, 37, 53, 128, 132, 151, 186.
Gordon, Max, 174.
Greene, Jimmy, 130.
Griffin, Johnny, 136, 187.
Guardian, newspaper, 175.
Hancock, Herbie, 85, 88-9.
Hardman, Bill, 30-31, 35, 43, 179.
Hargrove, Roy, 146-7, 187.
Harris, Barry, 35.
Harrison, Jim, 58.
Hartford, University, 110, 114-5, 123, 167, 173, 177, 185, 189.
  Hartt School, 111, 114-6, 124-5, 135, 166-8, 189.
HARYOU–ACT Harlem Youth Opportunities Unlimited–Associated Community Teams, 95, 99-100, 103, 110.

Hawkins, Coleman, 6, 8, 148, 155.
Haynes, Roy, 90, 92, 97, 136-7, 145, 184, 186-7.
Heath, Albert Tootie, 21.
Heath, Jimmy, 176.
Heath, Percy, 15.
Henderson, Eddie, 114.
Hentoff, Nat, 8, 31, 45, 98-100, 106.
Higgins, Billy, 65-6, 69-76, 105-6, 109, 118, 123-4, 128, 153-4, 159-61, 168, 172, 182-3, 185.
Hill, Andrew, 72.
Hill, Teddy, 7, 10.
Hodges, Johnny, 78, 155-6.
Holiday, Billie, 5-6, 36, 150.
Holt, Scotty, 105-6, 109, 120.
Hope, Elmo, 25, 178, 183.
Hubbard, Freddie, 59-61, 65, 175, 182.
Humphries, Lex, 181.
Hutcherson, Bobby, 83-5, 89, 91-2, 98, 120, 144, 154.
Jackie McLean on Mars, film, 100, 112, 114-5, 122, 129, 189-90.
Jackson, Milt, 19, 84, 114.
Jamal, Ahmad, 114.
James, Michael, 46-7, 64, 76-8, 158.
Jarvis, Clifford, 101-2.
Jazz Monthly, 46, 76.
Jazz Portraits, radio programme, 111, 123, 127, 129.
Jazz Times, 152, 169, 172.
Jazz Workshop club, San Francisco, 66, 75, 182.

Jazzhus Montmartre club, Copenhagen, 128, 186.
Jeffrey, Paul, 115.
Jenkins, Willard, 169.
Johnson, J. J., 14, 178.
Jones, Elvin, 41, 69, 90, 180.
Jones, Hank, 132, 186.
Jones, Philly Joe, 24, 35, 41, 45, 55, 76, 179-80.
Joplin, Scott, 191.
Jordan, Duke, 117, 136-7, 145, 186-7.
Kennedy, President John F. K., 103.
Kennedy, Robert, 100, 104.
Khan, Eddie, 83-85, 91.
King, Records, 180.
King, Martin Luther, 103-4.
Kirk, Andy, Jr., 5, 9.
Koenigswarter, Nica De, 64, 163.
Konitz, Lee, 142, 155, 185.
Korall, Burt, 41.
Lacy, Steve, 78.
Lamont, Johnson, 105-6, 109, 120.
Land, Harold, 183.
LaRoca, Pete, 48, 59-61, 180-2.
Lehman, Steve, 100, 102, 111, 122, 130.
Lewis, Herbie, 66, 89, 133, 144, 154, 183.
Liberty Records, 85, 88, 104, 117, 119.
Lincoln, Abbey, 102.
Lion, Alfred, 44, 59, 66, 70, 86, 88-90, 92, 104, 117, 119.

Little, Booker, 92.
Living Theatre Company, 48, 52, 95.
Lonehill Jazz Records, 38, 180.
Los Angeles Times, 148.
Mack, Charlie, 20-1.
Mariano, Charlie, 132, 185.
Marsalis, Wynton, 114.
Mattos, Michael, 53, 181.
McGhee, Howard, 53.
McLean, Alpha Omega, 7.
McLean, Dollie, 6, 16, 29, 33, 39, 94, 114, 116, 119, 123-4, 126-8, 138-40, 166, 175.
McLean, John, Sr, 7.
Mclean, Melonae, 21, 31, 33, 39, 50, 69, 126, 140, 189-90.
McLean, Rene, 33, 39, 49, 68, 77, 100, 126, 130-5, 152, 186.
McLean, Vernon, 39, 100.
McPherson, Eric, 146, 152.
Metronome magazine, 46.
Mingus, Charles, 13, 26-30, 34, 40, 42-3, 46, 56, 67, 112, 115, 156, 179-80.
Mitchell, Blue, 57, 61, 78, 118, 180, 185.
Mobley, Hank, 30, 37, 59, 118-9, 155, 157, 185.
Moncur III, Grachan, 72, 76, 81-3, 85-6, 89, 91, 93, 95, 105, 117, 144, 169.
Monk, Thelonious, 6, 22, 27, 64, 67, 72-3, 77, 113, 142, 163, 174, 176, 192.
Monterose, J. R., 26, 77.

INDEX

Morgan, Lee, 41, 61, 65, 77, 88, 96-7, 105, 117-9, 121-2, 182, 184-5.
Morton, Jelly Roll, 111.
Moses, J. C., 75.
Mulligan, Gerry, 143.
National Endowment for the Arts, 167, 173.
Nelson, Steve, 146, 187.
Neves, John, 81.
New School University, 173.
New York Post, 163.
New York Times, 174.
Newkirk, Eunice, 176.
Open Door club, NYC, 138, 163-4.
Pacific Jazz Records, 66-7, 182.
Palmer, Alan Jay, 145-146, 152.
Parker, Chan, 143.
Parker, Charlie, 1-6, 9-10, 12-23, 25, 27-8, 31, 33, 36-7, 40, 43, 45, 47, 49-52, 57, 59, 67, 70, 73, 76-7, 79-80, 86-7, 90, 95, 99-100, 107, 112, 115, 117, 126, 133-4, 136-145, 147-8, 150-3, 155-8, 162-5, 169, 173, 178-9, 186-7.
Parlan, Horace, 93.
Payne, Cecil, 136, 186.
Pearson, Duke, 181.
Pedersen, Niels-Henning Ørsted, 132, 186.
Pepper, Art, 142.
Pettiford, Oscar, 14.
Phipps, Arthur, 34.
Pinter, Harold, 168.
Potter, Tommy, 12-13.
Powell, Adam Clayton, 175.
Powell, Bud, 5-6, 8, 10, 27, 65, 69, 72-3, 90, 115, 142.
Powell, Richie, 5, 8.
Prendergast, Dick, 58.
Prestige Records, 8, 12, 14, 25-6, 34-5, 37, 44, 59, 68, 77, 92, 144, 156, 165, 178-9, 187.
Progressive Records, 22, 178.
Public Broadcasting Service TV, 172.
Ra, Sun, 87.
RCA Victor Records, 117.
Redd, Freddie, 52-5, 181-2.
Redman, Don, 5.
Reeves, Nat, 133, 166, 176, 186.
Ridley, Larry, 91-2, 105, 121, 184.
Riel, Alex, 128, 132, 186.
Ritchie, Larry, 37-8, 53, 80, 181.
Roach, Max, 30, 83, 102, 114.
Rodney, Red, 141.
Rollins, Sonny, 5-6, 8-9, 12-15, 47, 49, 59, 61, 67, 77-8, 152-3, 155-6, 172, 178.
Santisi, Ray, 81.
Savoy Records, 41.
Shaw, Woody, 95, 120, 132.
Shepp, Archie, 102, 111.
Sickler, Don, 136, 186.
Sidran, Ben, 73-4, 127.
Silver, Horace, 24, 30, 74, 89, 120, 135, 141, 178.
Simcock, Gwilym, 192.
Sinatra, Frank, 36.
Singleton, Charlie, 12.

Slugs Saloon bar, NYC, 124, 189.
Smith, Jimmy, 93.
Smith, Teddy, 75.
Smith, Warren, 176.
Smith, Willie, 155.
Somethin' Else Records, 159, 187.
Spellman, A. B., 97-8, 106, 112, 170.
Star Records, 12.
Steeplechase Records, 128, 132.
Stewart, Zan, 148-50.
Stickler, Don, 186.
Stieff, Bo, 128.
Stitt, Sonny, 9, 20, 59, 142, 151, 156.
Stravinsky, Igor, 87.
Student Nonviolent Coordinating Committee, 103.
Susuki, Isao, 128.
Taylor, Art, 5, 8, 22, 25, 34-5, 50, 57, 59, 67, 72, 75-6, 78, 178, 180-1.
Taylor, Billy, 175.
Taylor, Cecil, 27, 67, 72, 87, 92, 107, 109, 185.
Terry, Sue, 166-8.
Thornbury, Will, 27-30, 133-5.
Timmons, Bobby, 67, 74.
Tolliver, Charles, 95, 99, 105-6, 121-2, 184.
Toshiba EMI Records, 180.
Travis, Jack, 38.
Triloka Records, 27, 145, 156, 175, 186.
Tucker, George, 37, 80, 178.

Tucker, Ronald, 20, 172, 178.
Turrentine, Stanley, 65, 93.
Turrentine, Tommy, 65, 93, 182.
Tyner, McCoy, 96, 132.
United Artists Records, 66-7, 74, 88, 104, 183.
Van Gelder, Rudy, 50, 57, 66, 70-71, 85, 90, 96, 98, 102, 107, 117-8, 145.
Vaughan, Sarah, 90.
Verve Records, 51, 172, 186.
Victor (Japanese) Records, 128.
Village Vanguard club, NYC, 172-4.
Vinnegar, Leroy, 72, 75.
Waldron, Mal, 20, 23, 34-5, 80, 128, 133, 178-9.
Waller, Fats, 111.
Wallington, George, 22-4, 26, 89, 165, 178.
Walton, Cedar, 97, 123, 149, 153, 159-60, 166, 172-3.
Warren, Butch, 65, 71-2, 75, 85, 88, 182.
Washington, Tyrone, 120.
Watkins, Doug, 20, 25, 29-30, 35, 59-61, 73-4, 76, 89, 172, 178, 181-2.
Watrous, Peter, 174.
Webster, Ben, 8, 38, 78, 151.
Weinstock, Bob, 179.
WGBH Radio, Boston, 111.
Williams, David, 159-60.
Williams, Raymond, 152.
Williams, Robbie, 192.
Williams, Tony, 72, 76, 81, 83-5, 88-90, 93, 95, 132, 144, 184, 186.

Willis, Larry, 95, 101-2, 105, 121, 176.
Wilson, Jack, 117-8, 185.
Wolff, Francis, 44, 92, 104, 117, 119.
Woods, Phil, 37, 86, 143, 156.
Workman, Reggie, 97.
WWUH radio, 166.
X, Malcolm, 104.
Young, Lester, 6, 8, 36-7, 69, 73, 90, 106, 148, 151, 155, 165, 169.
Young, Webster, 37, 180.

BOOKS ABOUT JAZZ
FROM NORTHWAY

Derek Ansell,
Workout: The Music of Hank Mobley

Peter King,
Flying High: A Jazz Life and Beyond

Mike Hennessey,
The Little Giant: The Story of Johnny Griffin

Alan Robertson,
Joe Harriott – Fire in His Soul, 2nd edition

Leslie Thompson with Jeffrey Green,
Swing from a Small Island

Coleridge Goode and Roger Cotterrell,
Bass Lines: A Life in Jazz

John Chilton,
Hot Jazz, Warm Feet

Ron Brown with Digby Fairweather,
Nat Gonella: A Life in Jazz

Ronnie Scott with Mike Hennessey,
Some of My Best Friends Are Blues

Graham Collier,
The Jazz Composer – Moving Music off the Paper

Alan Plater,
Doggin' Around

Chris Searle,
Forward Groove: Jazz and the Real World from Louis Armstrong to Gilad Atzmon.

Ian Carr,
Music Outside

Peter Vacher,
Soloists and Sidemen: American Jazz Stories

Jim Godbolt,
A History of Jazz in Britain 1919–50

Jim Godbolt,
All This and Many a Dog

Vic Ash,
I Blew It My Way: Bebop, Big Bands and Sinatra

Digby Fairweather,
Notes from a Jazz Life

Harry Gold,
Gold, Doubloons and Pieces of Eight

Also by Derek Ansell

Workout: The Music of Hank Mobley

Hank Mobley, unjustly neglected in his lifetime, played and recorded with the greatest legends of his era, such as Miles Davis, John Coltrane, Dizzy Gillespie and Art Blakey, helping to create some of their finest work.

His best recordings are classics, with his instantly identifiable sound and style, and constant musical inventiveness. Now, at last, most of his recorded legacy is available on CD and he is increasingly recognised as one of the major figures of modern jazz. This book, the first to be published about him, provides a detailed introduction to the tenor saxophonist and his music.

hardback (papercase) 186 pages
ISBN 978-09550908 8 2 2008
13.99

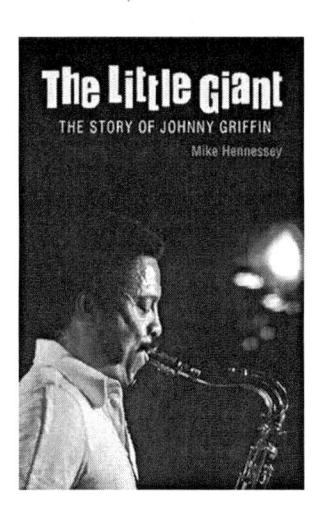

Mike Hennessey

The Little Giant: The Story of Johnny Griffin

Johnny Griffin, internationally recognized as a major jazz star, lived and worked in Chicago and New York before settling in Europe.

This biography includes reminiscences about his days with Lionel Hampton, Art Blakey, Thelonious Monk, Eddie 'Lockjaw' Davis, the Clarke–Boland Big Band and the groups he fronted in America and Europe during his sixty-two-year career as a tenor saxophonist.

An irreverent look back at the life of one of the most colourful and entertaining characters in jazz.

hardback with dust jacket, photos throughout   246 pages
ISBN 978-09550908 5 1   2008
£19.99

Join our mailing list for details of new books, events
and special offers: write to Northway Books,
39 Tytherton Road, London N19 4PZ, UK
email *info@northwaybooks.com*
or follow *Northway Jazz* on Twitter
www.northwaybooks.com